GOING HOME:

INFORMATION AND INSIGHTS ON
HOW TO PREPARE TO VISIT, REPATRIATE
OR LIVE AS AN EXPATRIATE IN AFRICA.

By Kofi Quaye

in collaboration with Peter Wynn and Godfred Mensah

authorHOUSE®

AuthorHouse™
1663 Liberty Drive
Bloomington, IN 47403
www.authorhouse.com
Phone: 1 (800) 839-8640

Published by AuthorHouse 11/22/2019

ISBN: 978-1-7283-3676-3 (sc)
ISBN: 978-1-7283-3675-6 (e)

DEDICATION

Dedicated to the Year of Return 2019 launched by President Nana Addo Dankwa Akuffo-Addo of Ghana, Lena Shockley [New York] the cast and production crew of 'COMING TO Africa' movie, Princess Angelique 'Ademiposi' Monet, Tashame Ali Hatten, [son] Ras Lawrence Davis, [Syracuse, NY] Carl Mensah, [London] Ocie Burton 11, [Las Vegas] Ayesha Quaye,[daughter] Trey Cotten. [son] George Kilpatrick, Berenice Teki Akuffo [New York] Regina Gilbert, Deborah Lacey, Edward Pincar, [New York] Charles Anderson [Syracuse] Bill Dewey, [Syracuse] Silas Sealmikky, [Lagos], Banji Oyemaja, [Lagos] and all the brothers and sisters I have met andinteracted with over the years. Africa awaits and will welcome and embrace all, especially people of African descent, who return to visit or to repatriate. This book has been researched and published with the goal of promoting closer ties between Africans and people of African heritage all over the world as embodied in the Year of Return initiative.

CONTENTS

THE NEW AFRICA

Books, travel brochures, magazines and other media describe Africa as the continent of unrivalled natural wonders, dramatic coastlines, amazing wildlife, luscious forests and unforgettable architecture.

Africa is also described in travel and tourism related media as a vast and highly diverse continent, full of pyramids and other ancient monuments, fascinating cultures, beautiful scenery, extraordinary animals and the best safari and wild game hunting in the world. As far as the travel and tourism industry is concerned, the image best suited for Africa is that of a tourist paradise, full of wide-ranging and exotic places.

For those interested in what may be considered as tourist attractions on the African continent, the above attributes make Africa the ideal place to visit.

It's not enough for those searching for information and data that will enable them to understand and relate to Africa and Africans on the basis of what is trending on the African continent in modern technology, communications, transportation, entertainment and recreation, the cultural sensibilities of the people, and how the different tribal and ethnic groups relate and interact with each other and with people from other continents.

AFRICA OFFERS MORE THAN SAFARIS, WILD GAME HUNTING AND ANCIENT MONUMENTS

Travel brochures and guidebooks about Africa do not contain pertinent information for those seeking to know more about Africa besides its tourist attractions. They don't concern themselves with disseminating solid, practical information and data that don't relate to the tourist packages that promote and publicize safaris, wild game watching and hunting and the great pyramids. That kind of information is not considered to be relevant or even necessary in part because they don't expect nor encourage people to experience anything else besides the pleasure of touring special places in Africa. Their focus is on promoting, publicizing and advertising traveling to Africa as an exciting adventure to an exotic and primitive continent, where they would tour places deemed to be relevant to the tourist experience, have meals in nice restaurants, sleep in luxury hotels and buy great gifts and souvenirs for friends and family back home in America or Europe.

The fact remains that many people from around the globe travel to Africa in search of more than the mere thrill of visiting a strange new place in an exotic environment. Many travel to Africa to pursue business interests. Others go there as expatriate employees of European and American conglomerates or nonprofit organizations or as business men and women exploring business opportunities. Lately, many African Americans and others of African descent from various parts of the world have traveled or are planning to travel to Africa to reconnect with the continent they consider as their ancestral homeland, many doing so with the goal of repatriating and living there on a permanent basis.

THIS BOOK FOCUSES ON PROVIDING USEFUL, RELEVANT AND PRACTICAL INFORMATION AND DATA ABOUT LIFE IN CONTEMPORARY AFRICA

It is to be expected that such people will be interested in accessing the kind of information and data that will give them a deeper insight and a better understanding of the culture, history, politics, social dynamics and other aspects of life on the African continent. This book focuses on that kind of travel experience and provides readers with information and data that will help them to understand and relate to the African continent and its people in a realistic manner.

While it is true that information and data about Africa may be available from the usual sources, it is also true that existing information and data might not necessarily contain what people are looking for, especially if they want to get a good grasp of current political, economic, financial and social developments and trends on the continent.

Travel brochures and guidebooks, for sure, will provide the usual information and data in a very superficial way. They definitely contain lots of information about interesting places to visit in Africa. Rarely do they focus seriously on the history, culture and contemporary lifestyles and other important aspects of life in Africa. The kind of information and data they put together is almost always a package that sells a trip to the continent of pyramids, safaris and wild game hunting. Getting a real understanding of the people is not particularly important to them. While that lopsided approach to presenting Africa to the rest of the world as a tourist paradise serves a purpose and a special clientele, it falls short in many ways, not the least of which is the fact that it doesn't tell the whole story.

Regardless of what motivates anyone to plan, consider or actually embark on a journey to Africa, it is absolutely necessary to be adequately prepared. This is the main reason for the publication of this book. Our goal is to do more than the travel related publications, books and the global media when it comes to presenting Africa to the world; to provide readers with real insight, valuable information and data on current trends in Africa as they relate to the history, culture, and other areas of life with the aim of making it a lot easier for them to have a better understanding of Africa and Africans.

CHAPTER ONE

COMMON STEREOTYPES, MISCONCEPTIONS AND MYTHS ABOUT AFRICA AND AFRICANS; PAST AND PRESENT

Nothing indicates the depth and scope of ignorance and misinformation about Africa more than the spate of misconceptions and stereotypes that have been created and hyped around the globe, giving the African continent and its people certain characteristics that have no basis in fact. As a result, the African continent is perceived as a less than ideal place to travel to as an expatriate or repatriate to even for people of African descent from America and elsewhere around the globe.

The misconceptions and stereotypes cover all aspects of life on the African continent, ranging from the languages and dialects to the general lifestyle of the people to how they relate to people from other races and the outside world.

According to global media hype, Africa is a dangerous, mysterious, undeveloped, disease ridden continent with a perpetually unstable political environment, inept leaders, corrupt governments, dysfunctional bureaucracies, ineffective corporate and financial structures, and unreliable information and communications technologies. Critics of coverage of Africa by the global media have made efforts to try to raise awareness about the need to present the right information and data about Africa to the world. They have also blamed the global media for playing a major role in projecting a negative image of Africa in part because they seem to focus more on the negative aspects of life on the African continent. Whether the global media will become more sensitive to the need to project a more positive image of Africa is not easy to determine. The debate continues. Meanwhile, the hype, misinformation and wrong data make it easy for people from other continents to come to the conclusion that nothing good comes out of Africa.

MISREPRESENTATION OF AFRICA IN BOOKS AND OTHER MEDIA ON A GLOBAL BASIS

For instance, books, articles, films and movies have been written, produced and published about Africa that have been proven to be lacking in substance and not wholly accurate in what they purport to write about. As a result, they continue to add to the confusion, ignorance and misinformation about Africa that project the African continent in the worst possible terms.

A glaring example is the media hype and coverage of the famine tragedy that befell certain parts of the African continent in the eighties and nineties and continues today in varying degrees. The global media led efforts to disseminate information and educate the global community about the gravity of the problem, but did it in a manner that presented it in seriously disturbing terms. Pictures of starving Africans that accompanied the stories not only created awareness of the famine and hunger situation, they created the impression that Africa is a continent in crisis politically, socially, economically and financially. Usually presented in the context of Africa as a continent that has more arable farming land than all the other continents, the coverage of the crisis in the global media raised serious and disturbing questions about the apparent inability of Africans to feed themselves, when they have all the resources needed to do so.

As part of the efforts to provide the global audience with information and data about the seriousness of the famine situation, the global media published pictures of starving African men and women with bulging, lifeless eyes staring out of sunken eye sockets, children with bloated stomachs who looked decades older than their actual years, crowds of desperate and hungry people stampeding towards trucks and helicopters that were dropping food and medical supplies donated by international humanitarian organizations to remote places. These were some of the images the global media published in newspapers, magazines, and on television all over the world about the African famine. It was no surprise that those images made a huge impact on world leaders and organizations that had the resources and influenced them to respond to appeals for help. At the same time, the same images lingered in the minds of the public as representing some of the attributes of Africa as a continent with poverty stricken people who cannot feed themselves and rely on outside aid for everything. Even after the crisis was over, at least the worst part of it, the tendency to associate the African continent with hunger, starvation and famine continued when the truth of the matter is that not all of Africa was affected. The media hype made the issue of hunger, starvation, famine in Africa a crisis for the global community to deal with, but the same media coverage reinforced the notion that the African continent is in chaos and helpless.

AFRICA AND AFRICANS HAVE TO DEAL WITH A HOSTILE GLOBAL MEDIA WHO HAVE NO INTEREST IN PROJECTING A POSITIVE IMAGE OF AFRICA AND AFRICANS TO THE WORLD

The misrepresentation, misconceptions and stereotyping of Africa and Africans continue to exist and spread as a result of what many Africans describe as a hostile global media that have shown a remarkable lack of interest in setting the record straight when it comes to reporting on trends in Africa. They just can't seem to be able to find anything good or positive to report about Africa, or so it seems. Efforts have been made by African leaders, governments, organizations and individuals that advocate on behalf of Africa and Africans to draw the attention of the global media to the adverse impact of the negative portrayal of Africa and Africans in the global media over the years, all to no avail.

It's been argued that it won't be easy to change the way the global media covers the African continent partly because it is not in their best interest, nor do they have any compelling reason to do so. It will change only when Africans take control of the narrative, which is a huge undertaking, and not likely to happen anytime soon. Interestingly enough, that may be happening to a certain degree, with the Internet and on social media. Facebook and other social media have become favorite outlets for people, organizations and even governments who seek to disseminate information and data that inform, educate and create awareness about issues relating to Africa, from a different perspective and in ways that present Africa and Africans in a more positive light to the rest of the world.

It is important that people traveling to Africa have an idea as to what is real and what is not in terms of what they know or have learned about the continent from sources available to them, especially regarding certain stereotypes and misconceptions. Again, stereotypes and misconceptions about Africa underscore the fact that it is a continent that has been the subject of all kinds of hype, misinformation and stereotyping as a result of people not being able to understand and relate to its history, politics, culture and other things. In this chapter, we'll deal with some of the more popular stereotypes and misconceptions about Africa, particularly those that most people seeking information about Africa are likely to encounter. We'll try to separate the facts from the myths, beginning with the most common: Africa is one large country.

AFRICA IS NOT ONE COUNTRY

Africa is not one large country. This is one of the most common misconceptions and stereotypes about Africa. For reasons that are not easy to explain, the notion of Africa as a country seems to be more plausible than the fact that it is a continent, that the entire continent is not one large country. Africa is a continent that consists of 54 countries. The various countries differ in sizes, populations and natural resources and have their own political, social and economic structures. Like other continents, the African continent has changed over time as a result of the impact of global politics, international commerce and trade, technological advancement and innovation. Great kings and chiefs have created and ruled over great empires: so have modern day politicians with ambitious plans to change the world and their people as well as traditional institutions and cultures that have been practiced for centuries and are still very much alive. It is a continent with different countries that have tried to develop their economies, adapt to changing times and provide their people with various forms of political systems as part of the ongoing process of being part of the modern world. How successful they have been or not is another story.

The point being made is this: Africa is a continent consisting of several sovereign nations with different forms of political systems, governmental machineries and national leaders. Africa is, in fact, larger in area than the USA, China, India, Japan and all of Europe combined.

AFRICAN COUNTRIES BORDERS WERE ARBITRARILY DRAWN AND IMPOSED ON THEM BY EUROPEAN COUNTRIES IN THE BERLIN CONFERENCE OF 1884

The only dispute about the territoriality of African nations is the way the borders between most African countries were drawn and the effect they have had on the continent politically, socially, economically and financially. The borders of most African countries were arbitrarily drawn and imposed on them by European countries at the Berlin Conference of 1884. It marked the climax of a period in history often referred to as the Scramble for Africa, a period during which many European countries such as Great Britain, France, and Germany began to focus on Africa as the source for natural resources for their growing industrial sectors as well as a potential market for the goods their factories produced.

As a result, they sought to safeguard their commercial interests in Africa and began sending scouts to the continent to secure treaties from indigenous people that were supposed to give them access to and ownership of territories on the African continent. King Leopold II of Belgium who aspired to increase his personal wealth by acquiring African territory, hired agents to lay claim to vast tracts of land in Central Africa. Germany did the same. German Chancellor Otto von Bismarck, felt compelled to make claims to African land, to protect his country's commercial interests.

Inevitably, the scramble for territory led to conflict among the European powers, particularly the British and French in West Africa, the Portuguese and British in East Africa, and the French and the Belgians in Central Africa. Rivalry between Great Britain and France played a huge role in creating the need for mediation. In 1884, Germany's Otto von Bismarck called a meeting of the European powers in Berlin that included Great Britain, France, Germany, Portugal, and Belgium at which they negotiated their claims to African territory, which were then formalized and mapped with no input from the African countries. Referred to as an arbitrary and illegal demarcation of Africa by foreign governments, it remains a controversial issue in African politics, and is blamed for creating serious problems that have not been easy to deal with. The political instability, civic unrest and chaos, tribal conflicts, internecine wars, economic underdevelopment and other serious problems Africa and Africans have faced in the past and continue to deal with have been blamed on the arbitrary borders drawn and imposed on them by European governments that divided tribes, communities, and countries.

The result was nothing short of chaos. Tribes, cities, towns, villages and even families were divided, creating countries with people who had been separated from communities they belonged to before the partition. For instance, in Ghana, the outer part of the eastern half of the country is occupied by the Ewe tribe. The neighboring country of Togoland has a tribe with language, traditions, customs and other characteristics that are the same or similar to those practiced by the Ewe tribe in Ghana. The obvious conclusion is that they were once a large tribe that lived as a cohesive tribal community. The partitioning of Africa by the European powers in 1884 sliced them into pieces, placing half in Ghana, the other half in Togo and others in Benin. African leaders, journalists and advocates on Africa related issues have argued that the borders of African countries as they currently exist are fundamentally flawed in light of the fact that they were arbitrarily imposed on them by Europeans who had little or no knowledge about the African continent.

ALL AFRICANS DON'T SPEAK ONE LANGUAGE

Africans communicate with each other by way of a highly diversified and complex system of languages. It is a huge mistake for anyone to assume they speak one language simply because they don't understand what is being said or that they sound the same. There is absolutely nothing like one common language that is spoken and understood by everyone in all of Africa. It is a continent of multiple languages. The various tribes and ethnic groups are usually identified by the language spoken by that particular group, though it is not unusual to find two different languages spoken in two different communities only a few miles apart. It has been estimated that there are over 2,000 languages in Africa. Certain countries like Nigeria have over 200 different languages spoken by as many tribal groups. However, it is important to note that there are some languages that are spoken across many countries. For instance, Swahili is the dominant language in most of East Africa. Anyone conversant in that language will find it a lot easier to navigate the cultural and social landscape in that part of Africa. So is Zulu in Southern Africa, among others. To a certain degree, the Hausa language may fit into the category of being the dominant language in most areas of West Africa. It is present in varying forms in most West African countries including Nigeria, Ghana, Ivory Coast, Burkina Faso, Mali and others. Regardless, none of those have the attributes of a major language for it to be described as the universal African language.

AFRICANS LEARN ENGLISH AND FRENCH IN SCHOOL AND CAN SPEAK AND WRITE IN BOTH LANGUAGES. PORTUGUESE AND SPANISH ARE ALSO COMMON IN SOME AFRICAN COUNTRIES

Africa has, in fact, been described as the most multilingual continent in the world. It is not rare for individuals to fluently speak not only multiple African languages, but one or more European languages as well.

Quite often, people from other continents seem to be both surprised and amused when they encounter Africans who seem to have no problem expressing themselves in English with British and American accents. These are natives of countries in West, East, North and South Africa who have been exposed to British influence as a result of their colonial past. In countries such as Ghana and Sierra Leone and other West African countries, English is spoken and used as often and sometimes more than the local dialects. English is taught in schools and is the official language in many African countries.

The same applies to the French language. A considerable number of Africans have the ability to communicate in French, also a legacy from colonial times when a number of African countries were under French rule. Those countries in Africa where French is spoken are referred to as the Francophone zone. English speaking African countries constitute the Anglophone zone. The only flaw may be their inability to get the British and French accents right.

The good news for anyone traveling to Africa these days is that the multiplicity of languages in African countries does not present a problem. English and French, the two dominant global languages are widely spoken all over the continent of Africa. Anyone conversant in either language will find it easy to navigate their way through most situations in Africa, regardless of the reason for going there. To a lesser extent, but spoken in a significant number of African countries are Portuguese, Spanish and German.

The fact that there are multiple languages in most African countries suggests that there's nothing like one African culture or language. It also makes it necessary for Africans to find a common language they can all use to communicate such as Portuguese in Mozambique and French in Guinea. These European languages have become well established and in some instances have been adopted as the official language.

WILD ANIMALS AND AFRICAN PEOPLE DON'T LIVE TOGETHER

The majority of Africans have to go to a zoo to see wild animals like lions, leopards and hyenas, just like other people in cities around the globe. Coming in contact in any fashion with wild animals in Africa is not as common an experience as most people think. Most Africans rarely see wild animals, particularly those who live in cities and urban townships. Urbanized areas are usually devoid of wild animals, unless they are housed and exhibited in zoos to people who have to go there to see the wild animals in captivity.

As a result of the misconceptions and stereotypes about Africa, people tend to believe that Africans and wild animals live together, that wild animals such as lions, leopards, and hyenas are kept as pets in the communities in which they live. They make it seem like wild animals live in close proximity or with the people. It is true that large numbers of Africans, especially those in the rural areas, live close to nature, which basically means they sustain themselves largely by farming the land, hunting game, fishing in the rivers, and harnessing the resources nature has provided them. Even under those circumstances, wild animals don't live in their midst as suggested by one of the most common misconceptions about Africa and Africans. Wild animals pose the same danger to them like they do elsewhere to people in other parts of the world.

ALL AFRICANS DON'T LIVE IN HUTS AND MUD HOUSES

Thatched huts made of mud and dung have been featured in books, documentary films and movies, television news stories and newspaper articles as living quarters of certain tribes of people in Africa. That image has stuck with people over the years to the degree where many simply assume that is standard housing in most African countries, even in this modern age. The real picture is a lot different. Africa has moved right along into the modern era with cities that contain some of the most spectacular buildings to be found anywhere on the globe. Many African nations have launched and are implementing ambitious development programs that include the creation of modern housing facilities, office buildings, hotels and other edifices in cities, townships, residential areas and neighborhoods. Walking through some downtown areas in many African cities, the infrastructure, streets and other city sights might not seem to be any different. There are broad boulevards with malls, shopping centers, dual carriageways, and all kinds of infrastructure that make it easy for people and vehicles to move from one area to another. Evidence of the enormous growth and development in Africa are communities with brick and stone houses, clean tap water, internet connectivity and electricity, as well as other basic necessities that are accessible to residents in some of the world's best cities. Huts were the most common forms of housing in rural areas on the continent in the past, but the trend now is the construction of modern houses in the cities, towns and villages. Many African cities have beautifully designed skyscrapers and other infrastructure that are similar to those to be found in most cities around the world.

MODERN TECHNOLOGIES EXIST AND THRIVE IN AFRICA

African immigrants who live overseas return to their countries to find out that their folks back home are not missing out on the benefits of the technological advancements that have taken place in Europe, America and elsewhere. They find out quickly that the digital age has had a huge impact in Africa. More importantly, their family and friends back home tend to be more tech savvy with electronic gadgets, and appear to know more about smartphones, computers and laptops. The folks back home who have not set foot outside the confines of their countries seem to be better equipped and more adept at handling complex tasks with smartphones, computers and laptops. Quite often, African immigrants in Europe and America who go back home have to pick up hints and tips on how to gain access to and maximize their use of apps that make it possible for them to make free phone calls to different parts of the world, send emails, access certain websites to get specialized information to promote their businesses, market and sell merchandise, make friends and interact with online contacts all over the world, all at little or no cost. Access to Wi-Fi is the key. And that is not a problem in Africa today.

Interestingly enough, most of them have not had any specialized kind of training in any field. Their knowledge and expertise come from converting access to technology to multiple applications, learning how to use and manipulate them by way of experimentation and a common sense approach to finding ways to get more out of available resources. The widespread use of apps such as WhatsApp in Africa has been cited in the global media as evidence that Africa and Africans are right up there with the rest of the world when it comes to the use of existing technologies for communication, education, and dissemination of information and data.

This clearly demonstrates that modern technology is widely used and available in Africa, contrary to what people have been led to believe, that the continent lacks modern technology. No matter where you happen to travel to in Africa these days, be it in the remotest village in deep rural areas or an isolated beach somewhere, access to technology is possible.

The numbers speak for themselves. According to statistics compiled by a leading agency that monitors technological trends around the world, Africa is among the leading continents in mobile phone use. It is estimated that over 67% of the population on the continent have mobile phones, and 27% have a device that can access the internet, making it the region with the fastest growth in the use of mobile phone technology. 27% of the total population of Africa have tablets at their disposal. Access to and use of technology is widespread in Africa and is projected to continue to increase and expand.

ALL AFRICANS ARE NOT DARK SKINNED

Jim Miller is tall and blonde with blue eyes. Nothing about him suggests he's anything other than what he looks like: a white man with all the classic attributes of the human race often referred to as Caucasians. He travels quite a bit and every time he shows his passport, the reaction is the same: confusion. For obvious reasons, people seem to be confused at the idea of a white African. They simply cannot reconcile Africa with a white person. All Africans are supposed to be dark skinned. The truth is that white Africans are a fact of life. In many African countries, white Africans make up a significant portion of the native population and claim African citizenship like the rest of the Africans. Many claim to belong to families that have lived in Africa for several generations, giving them the right to demand to be recognized as legitimate Africans with all the rights and privileges of citizenship. African countries in which white Africans remain an important minority include Zimbabwe, Namibia and South Africa, often referred to as the Rainbow Nation because of the diversity it is known for when it comes to matters of skin color.

The Dutch and British represent the largest communities of European ancestry in Southern Africa, with smaller communities of people of French and German ancestry in other parts of the continent.

European colonization also brought sizable groups of Asians, particularly from the Indian subcontinent to African countries that were British colonies before they attained independence. Large Indian communities are found in South Africa, and smaller ones are present in Kenya, Tanzania, and some other southern and southeast African countries. The large Indian community in Uganda was expelled by President Iddi Amin in 1972 when it was determined that the presence of a large number of Indians was not in the best interest of the country. Media reports indicate that many have since returned. The islands in the Indian Ocean are also populated primarily by people of Asian origin, often mixed with Africans and Europeans. Along the coast, the population is generally mixed with people of Bantu, Arab, Indian and European origins. Malay and Indian ancestries are also important components in the group of people known in South Africa as Cape Colored's. It refers to people with origins in two or more races and continents. During the 20th century, small but economically important communities of Lebanese and Chinese developed in the larger coastal cities of West and East Africa and are expanding rapidly.

AFRICA HAS PRODUCED OUTSTANDING LEADERS RECOGNIZED FOR THEIR GREAT LEADERSHIP QUALITIES

When Iddi Amin emerged as the leader of Uganda, he moved to the center stage of global politics and rose to infamy as one of the most brutal dictators of his time, at least that was how he was portrayed in the global media. He seemed to take particular delight in making statements that derided leaders of Europe and America and taking actions that antagonized them and other world leaders. Not surprisingly, the global media focused considerable attention on him and made every effort to cover and publicize everything he did. During his era and long after he made his exit from the political arena, the image of Iddi Amin as the mad, brutal dictator lingered around the world. With a global media that continued to focus on the negative aspects of life in Africa, the Iddi Amin story contributed to creating the notion that African leaders are corrupt, inept and lacking in political sophistication.

On the other hand, Nelson Mandela of South Africa has emerged as one of the most recognized and respected world leaders in recent memory. Revered for his courage, genial personality, integrity and statesmanship, he gained the respect of American presidents and other world leaders. Corruption was not one of his virtues.

Other African leaders have also gained global recognition on the basis of their outstanding leadership qualities. One such African leader was Dr Kwame Nkrumah of Ghana. He led his country to independence in 1957, making Ghana the first African nation south of the Sahara Desert to achieve independence. He became known for his relentless commitment to fighting for the development of his country and the unification of Africa, and appeared not to have amassed any sizeable personal fortune. Yet the uprightness of Nkrumah and the courage and personal integrity of Mandela have not been as widely publicized and hyped as the notoriety of corrupt African leaders and politicians. Indeed, the global media's fascination with what they describe as the corrupt and strongman tactics of Iddi Amin, Gaddafi, Robert Mugabe and other African leaders have reinforced the notion that corruption is rife in Africa, beginning at the top.

Critics of media coverage of Africa and its impact on the image of Africa continue to blame the global media for having the tendency to misrepresent Africa when it comes to reporting trends and activities on the African continent. In recent times, social media has proven to be a valuable source of information and data about Africa. Digital journalists, bloggers, websites, and many other social media platforms have made extensive use of the Internet to publish, promote books, documentaries, films, and online publications that project Africa as a continent with potential for development in all areas of life. Many who describe themselves as Pan Africanists have made no secret of their willingness and readiness to use social media in their efforts to project Africa in a positive light to the world. They are unapologetically pro Africa and have committed themselves to portraying Africa as a rich continent that has been exploited by Europeans and Americans. They put all the blame where they think it belongs: forces outside Africa that have exploited the continent for centuries and continue to do so in many ways.

AFRICA IS NOT A DESERT: IT HAS THE LARGEST DESERT IN THE WORLD

The Sahara Desert is the largest desert in the entire world and covers more square miles than the entire United States of America. It is in Africa. Other deserts in Africa are the Kalahari and Namib Deserts. The Sahara Desert by itself, occupies about one third of Africa. The combined area covered by the various deserts is so huge that it is possible that it created another misconception about Africa when it is mistakenly presumed to be a continent largely occupied by a desert called the Sahara. The huge deserts of Africa have been described as being key to making the continent unique and distinct, but that does not make Africa a desert continent.

The sandy dunes of the Sahara and other deserts contrast sharply with another of nature's wonders in Africa: luscious vegetation and tropical rain forests that cover large areas of the continent and are used for farming and are home to a wide variety of fauna and flora not found anywhere else. Africa has been credited with having the most flourishing wildlife in the entire world, making it a leading attraction for tourists with interest in nature and wildlife.

AFRICANS DON'T SHARE A HOMOGENOUS CULTURE: ALL AFRICAN CULTURES ARE NOT THE SAME

Media portrayal of African culture has been the iconic image of Africans whose faces are covered with a distinctive red paint with mud huts and thatched roofs in the background. The people are known as the Red People. That image has been featured in most of the major travel magazines, newspapers and publications that showcase the different tribes of the world and the unique cultural characteristics attributed to them. For Africa, this particular image appears to capture the essence of African culture to Europeans and Americans who know little or nothing about African culture and seems to have contributed significantly to creating the misconception that Africa and Africans have one culture. That the iconic image of people with their faces painted red has made the most impact is beyond question. The fact remains though that the powerful and iconic image does not represent the culture of the entire African continent. The Red People constitute only one tribe in the southern part of Africa. Africa has over 2000 tribal groups that have widely differing cultural traditions, making African countries the most diverse in terms of the multiplicity of tribes, languages and cultures. According to studies on the ethnic diversity of Africa in relation to other continents, Africa is by far the most culturally diverse continent with no two countries governed by the same culture. Each ethnic or tribal group has its own unique set of cultural beliefs that provide them with the cultural norms and traditions often showcased through dress code, piercings, skin marking, and food, as well as other tribal practices. Ironically, the only thing close to cultural homogeneity in Africa seems to be Western influence. The impact of Western influence in Africa is evident in all aspects of life, especially when it relates to the younger generation. The music, the fashion, entertainment, movies and almost everything else in metropolitan areas in most African countries are based on European and American models, a trend that has been observed all over the continent.

As a result, indigenous African cultures tend to be less visible in cities and are not a common sight in most urban settings partly because the majority of the people in the metropolitan areas gravitate towards a lifestyle that is supposed to be trending around the world, usually imposed on them by other cultures from outside Africa.

In other words, the cultural sensibilities of Africans, particularly the younger generation in cities tend to be based on lifestyle models that have little or nothing to do with Africa. Consequently, the younger generation behave in ways that portray them as being part of the modern global community, a world that is totally different.

CHANGING DEMOGRAPHICS IN AFRICA

The demographics of Africa is changing rapidly, reflecting a transition from rural based small sized communities to huge metropolitan areas that have huge concentrations of people from different parts of the various countries. The rural lifestyle has lost its appeal, particularly to the younger generation that has received education and can't find jobs that make use of the skills and abilities they have developed. They migrate to the cities looking for jobs, pursuing education, searching for and exploring opportunities in business, the arts and entertainment. Dispersed over wide areas, the people from the various tribes no longer live in close proximity to each other, don't speak their tribal languages for the most part, and have no compelling reason to adhere to the customs and traditions in the new urban environment. The prevailing lifestyle in those environments differs from what they have known in their rural communities. The result is the emergence of a subculture that is a mixture of everything foreign to them, but appealing simply because it creates a sense of being current and in tune with what's trending out there in the rest of the world. Access to the Internet and other modern information and communication technologies has played a significant role in exposing Africans to European and American cultural influences, making it a lot easier for those cultures to have an impact on city dwellers in African countries, particularly the younger generation. It also explains why the younger generation tends to be more inclined to assimilating the lifestyles of people foreign to the continent. They are exposed to various aspects of western culture, in the form of the fashion, music, entertainment and artistic creations that are all too common on the Internet and other media these days. It is quite possible to run into someone in Accra in Ghana or Lagos in Nigeria whose attire, attitude, and sometimes even manner of speaking might not be significantly different from someone his or her age in a city in America or Europe. Their new lifestyle comes with the pressure to keep up with the trends they see in movies, on television and lately in social media. And quite often, they have little or nothing to do with Africa and Africans.

ALL AFRICAN COUNTRIES ARE NOT POOR. NEITHER DO THEY ALL DEPEND ON AID FROM AMERICA AND EUROPE

The African continent is not considered poor if the determination is based on its natural resources. It is rich in natural resources of all types and has been the source of raw materials that have been used to manufacture a whole variety of products that are sold all over the world.

The continent of Africa has extensive reserves of oil and is the world's fastest-growing region for foreign direct investment. It has approximately 30 percent of the earth's remaining mineral resources. These include cobalt, uranium, diamonds and gold, as well as significant oil and gas reserves.

The Democratic Republic of Congo has one of the richest deposits of mineral resources that include copper, cobalt, diamonds, oil, coltan, gold, and tin.

The mining industry in Africa is expansive and covers a broad spectrum of minerals that are exported to foreign countries and converted into other products used all over the world. Africa produces at least 50% of the diamonds and gold in the whole world. The rest of the countries around the world contribute to the remaining 50% of the production of these precious stones and metals. Nigeria is Africa's largest oil producing country. Botswana and South Africa are the most economically developed regions. Agriculture is considered the continent's single most important economic activity and employs two-thirds of the continent's working population and contributes 20 to 60 percent of every country's gross domestic product

The misrepresentation, misconceptions and stereotyping of Africa and Africans as poor is the result of the role played by a hostile global media that seems to have no interest in setting the record straight when it comes to reporting on Africa.

FOREIGN AID TO AFRICA DOES NOT SOLVE ALL THEIR PROBLEMS: AFRICAN LEADERS ARE MAKING THE EFFORT TO BE LESS DEPENDENT ON FOREIGN AID

Like the rest of the developing countries around the globe, aid from foreign countries to African countries plays a significant role in allowing governments to deliver services such as water, sanitation services and education more than they would otherwise be able to do.

African leaders have encouraged investments in human capital development with the expectation that they will deliver large benefits and have long term positive effects. They have also placed a high priority on implementing government policies that would ultimately make them less dependent on foreign aid. The goal is to make the continent self-sufficient and able to sustain the economies of the various countries without depending on foreign aid. Ghana's Nana Akuffo-Addo has emerged as a leading figure in articulating the need for African countries to be less dependent on foreign aid. Elected to office in 2016, he has been on the frontline in the campaign to attain the goal of eliminating the need for foreign aid in Ghana and Africa. He has stated on several occasions that African countries have the potential to develop and sustain themselves to a point where there would be no need to depend on foreign aid. Many African leaders share his vision, have embraced the notion of economic independence for African countries and have indicated their readiness to work together to become self-reliant, self-sufficient and potentially nondependent on foreign aid from Europe and America.

FASCINATING FACTS ABOUT AFRICA

Considered by many scientists to be the origin of mankind, life as we know it began and evolved in Africa. Africa is the root of all mankind, making it the oldest continent. Fossil remains found in Africa indicate that it is the first continent where humans lived. The fossil remains have suggested that humans inhabited the African continent around 7 million years ago.

Africa is considered to be the second largest continent in the world with a total area of around 11 million square miles that account for 5.7% of the earth's surface as well as 20% of the total surface of land on our planet.

It has a rich geography, widespread biodiversity as well as a fascinating history. Africa has much more to it than the poverty for which it is well known the world over.

THERE ARE 54 COUNTRIES IN AFRICA

There are 54 countries in Africa. Sudan used to be the largest country until it was split into Sudan and South Sudan. Algeria is now the largest African country based on the geographical area it occupies.

THE CLIMATE OF AFRICA

The climate in Africa is generally described as tropical, suggesting that it is hot, humid and wet. That is essentially true, but there are significant variations in the weather patterns that are caused by the same factors that regulate weather conditions all over the world. Some of the more interesting facts about the climate of Africa are the seasonal changes.

THE SEASONS IN AFRICA

Africa's position on the globe is the determining factor and is responsible for dividing the African continent into five different climate types.

Rainforest –This region is characterized by very high temperatures and high rainfall throughout the year.

Savanna – Like the rain forest, this region has very high temperatures all year but lacks the high rainfall of the rainforest. The rainy season of the savanna occurs during the summer season.

Steppe – This region has high temperatures all year and only limited rainfall during the summer season.

Desert – High temperatures throughout the year with very little rainfall.

Mediterranean – Warm to high temperatures with rainfall in the autumn and winter months.

CHAPTER TWO

HOW TO NAVIGATE THE DIFFERENT CULTURES AND TRADITIONS IN URBAN AND RURAL COMMUNITIES IN AFRICA

The notion that Africans have a genial and friendly disposition is essentially true. Anyone who has travelled to the African continent and interacted with Africans will bear testimony to their willingness and readiness to welcome and embrace other people, regardless of where they come from or what race they belong to.

This translates into an eagerness on their part to reach out and make friends wherever they happen to be and with whomever they come in contact with. It reflects, in most part, their common approach and way of relating to people: with open arms and a warm smile. It comes naturally to them in pretty much the same way that other people act in ways that seem to be innate to them in the environment in which they live when it comes to relating to strangers. Nurtured in a cultural environment that stresses trust in one's neighbor, it is an attitude that contrasts sharply with the way others react in similar situations in America, Europe and other countries.

People from other cultures, especially Europe and America tend to approach strangers with caution, if not suspicion, no matter where they happen to be. Strangers are kept at bay by way of hostile body language, unfriendly facial expressions and sometimes blatant in your face nastiness, regardless of where the encounters occur. It can be in the workplace, in the neighborhood, in the grocery store, in the park, the general attitude is one of alertness and vigilance.

If the man or woman trying to start a conversation does not seem familiar to you, the immediate reaction is to back off or just ignore him or her. For all you know, it could be a set-up, or a trick to divert your attention so you can be robbed or mugged, or killed. These are countries and cultures in which no one can take anything for granted. No matter where you happen to be, the specter of crime looms overhead, sometimes forcing people to live in a kind of permanent paranoia. It is the norm in such countries to have a mentality of being constantly alert and cautious all the time. They live in an environment where safety and security concerns call for a different approach.

READINESS TO EMBRACE AND WELCOME STRANGERS IS PART OF MOST AFRICAN CULTURES AND TRADITIONS

It is different in Africa. African cultures impart into the people a sense of community that permeates all aspects of life. They learn early to trust their neighbors and consider them as more than mere neighbors. Everyone in the community is perceived as a member of an extended family. The entire village or town is one big family.

Consequently, they are used to living in communities where trust is the norm, and everything they do underscores the underlying spirit of mutual trust that operates in such communities. For instance, it used to be a common practice to leave one's door open most of the time in the majority of African communities, especially in the rural areas. People cultivated the habit of leaving their doors unlocked and open if they have to leave the house for a short period to run to the store or do an errand. It was in fact, considered rude for anyone to show a tendency to close doors, especially when they were home. Thus if Africans seem to be friendly and open, it is because the spirit of friendliness is engendered in them early in life by the cultures in which they are born and raised.

It changes once they assimilate the city lifestyle and get to know of the risks one takes in talking to strangers or just being too friendly in the urban environment in large cities.

CHANGING LIFESTYLES IN AFRICAN COUNTRIES

Interestingly enough, in the major cities such as Lagos, Accra, Nairobi, Johannesburg, or Abidjan and in other large cities and urban areas elsewhere on the African continent, the lifestyle is similar to what exists in similar environments around the world. It is just as dangerous in these cities as it is in New York or Chicago, London or Berlin, if not more. People in certain parts of African cities are definitely not as open, friendly and trusting and most certainly do not leave their doors open when they leave home.

Large portions of these cities are modern, urbanized with high rise apartment buildings, skyscraper office buildings, airports and advanced technologies that connect them with other parts of the world, making them a part of the global marketplace with along with everything else that comes with it.

URBAN AND CITY LIFE IN AFRICAN COUNTRIES CAN BE DANGEROUS

The lifestyle in these cities is not too different from what one sees in urban settings around the globe. In these highly urbanized communities, the lifestyle has as its most striking characteristic, a close resemblance to what exists in any major city in America or in Europe: modern technology being used in different ways to facilitate commerce and trade of all kinds and at various levels, all aimed at making money by any means necessary and finding ways to spend it. Here, the pace of life is determined mostly by the demand and search for ways to gratify needs created by the new urban lifestyle that calls for better forms of transportation, communication, recreation and entertainment.

This is the lifestyle that has propelled some African cities such as Lagos into the limelight of international notoriety.

RURAL COMMUNITIES IN AFRICA ARE DIFFERENT FROM URBAN COMMUNITIES BECAUSE THEY RETAIN THE OLD LIFESTYLE IN WHICH BELIEF IN TRADITIONS, CUSTOMS AND SUPERSTITIONS DOMINATE

In the rural communities, away from the huge, sprawling urbanized cities, the lifestyle is different in many respects mostly, devoid of the pressures and demands that make life stressful in cities.

These are the villages and towns where the people live a relatively simple and uncomplicated lifestyle. They make an effort to retain most of the traditional beliefs, customs and norms that regulate the way they live their lives. In such small communities, the impact of modernization has been minimal, and has not done much to influence the local population in terms of cultivating patterns of behavior usually found in urban areas. Their approach to life is rooted in their native culture, their understanding of and relationship to nature and the forces that are assumed to have the power and ability to influence their lives. Their lifestyle is essentially a reflection of their way of life that inculcates into them a sense of what is right and wrong. These are cultures that have evolved their own ways of punishing those whose actions are judged to be wrong as well as rewarding those who do the right thing. They are cultures in which anyone caught stealing may be punished by having an arm cut off, so there wouldn't be an arm to use to steal again, and has proven to be quite effective in deterring others from stealing. In such communities, people might still leave their doors open when they have to run an errand that will not take them too far from their house.

Again, we are not able to discuss at length, the merits and demerits of the various cultures of Africa, or how effective or ineffective they are compared to other cultures. Suffice it to say that Africa, like other continents, has its different faces. It has the old and the new; the old with its entrenched customs and traditions, vigorously enforced by way of superstition and tradition and dutifully obeyed by the population. The lifestyle in these rural communities is essentially unaffected by modern civilization, very much what it has been over the centuries, inhabited by people who feel no inclination to change the way they live.

As for the new face of Africa, it is a brand new world created by the need to be a part of the global community, made possible by modern technology. It is characterized by huge cities coping with social, political and economic pressures brought on by overpopulation and over consumption. They are two totally different worlds that seem to co-exist and continue to function in ways that reinforce the fundamental differences between them, making the continent what it is and always will be; the oldest continent on earth that will change in many ways, yet remain the same in many ways as well.

UNANSWERED QUESTIONS ABOUT LIFE IN AFRICA

Many questions arise when it comes to discussing traveling to Africa regardless of the duration or the reason. They include speculations about which part of Africa will better accommodate African-Americans and others of African descent from other parts of the world who are repatriating to Africa considering the fact that most are born and raised in cities In Europe and America. Will they find the urbanized environment in major metropolitan areas easier to fit in or will they be drawn to the rural areas, away from the hustle and bustle of city life?

CHAPTER THREE

HOW SAFE IS AFRICA FOR VISITORS, EXPATRIATES AND THOSE REPATRIATING? IS THERE A SPECIAL WAY TO PREPARE TO TRAVEL TO AFRICA?

On April 3, 2019, breaking news announcement on American television stations and the BBC and other media outlets around the globe reported the grim news that an American tourist and her driver had been kidnapped in Uganda by Africans. The victim was named Kimberley Sue Endicott. The kidnapping had all the characteristics of a well-planned operation carried out with military precision. It occurred in a national park frequented by tourists and the victim was not alone. Traveling with other tourists, the kidnappers appeared to have targeted her and her driver. According to the news report, the Ugandan authorities had launched an investigation and had reason to believe that the situation would be resolved.

This was the kind of news no one wants to hear, certainly not the Ugandan government and tourists like Kimberley Sue Endicott who travel to Africa from other countries around the world with the expectation that they would enjoy their visit and return home safely.

The Ugandan government issued statements to the effect that every effort would be made to rescue the American tourist and apprehend the kidnappers. And that was precisely what happened.

A few days later, it was announced on American television that the American tourist and her driver had been freed from her captors and was on her way home. A number of Africans suspected to be involved in the kidnapping had been arrested and would be prosecuted to the fullest extent of the law. Investigations would continue as part of an ongoing process to reduce the possibility of such incidents occurring in the future.

In the wake of such an incident, it is a perfectly legitimate question for anyone planning to travel to the African continent for whatever reason to ask questions and express concern about security and safety. Will they be safe? Will they be secure? Will they be kidnapped? Will they be at risk in any way that can endanger their lives? How safe is it in Africa for anyone visiting, repatriating or becoming an expatriate with plans to live there on a permanent basis?

Let us begin with the notion that most people know little or nothing about Africa. That is usually the case with the majority of people traveling to Africa for the first time. More than likely, they have very limited information about Africa. That's not surprising, considering the fact that there is a lack of interest in the continent of Africa on the part of most people around the globe. Why should they? They don't have any compelling reasons to be interested in Africa or look for information about the African continent.

Thus Africa has little or no significance for those who are not directly linked to it in some fashion. When they do show interest and search for information and data, they look for information that will shed light on what they have been told or reinforce the usual stereotypical notions most foreigners tend to have about Africa. As alluded to elsewhere, the global media has contributed significantly to projecting an image of Africa and Africans that gives people every reason to make conclusions that turn them off.

To most people outside of Africa, the African continent is the land of primitive tribes, superstitious natives, poor, hungry people who have no idea about what's going on in the rest of the world. It is not true, but the global media continues to play a huge role in the dissemination of information that effectively makes Africa look like an unsafe continent.

Even though traveling in Africa is considered to be relatively safe, except in areas identified as conflict zones or susceptible to acts of terrorism, books and other media that discuss the subject tend to provide information and data that often seem to suggest otherwise. Our research indicates that is not the true story.

According to the Institute for Economics and Peace, which bases its rankings on such factors as violent crime, terrorism, and internal and external conflicts, many African countries provide an environment that is safer than the United States. They include Botswana, Namibia, Zambia, Madagascar, Ghana, Sierra Leone, Tanzania, and Malawi. Yet for reasons already pointed out, Africa and Africans continue to be perceived in ways that make it seem like it is the most dangerous and risky continent in the world.

PLACES IN AFRICA THAT ARE NOT SAFE

Again, it is an undeniable fact that certain areas in Africa have been in the news for incidents that provide evidence of the presence of terrorists committed to various causes. They seek and find targets to hit that make an impact and promote their cause as a result. Governments in control in those areas continue to take action to eliminate those threats and restore stability. It is in their interest to make their countries safe for tourists. Failure to do so gives outsiders reason to believe that they may not be safe in those countries. And quite often government intervention creates situations that lead to civil wars and other forms of conflicts. Thus wars, rebel activity, social and political conflicts can make travel unwise in certain areas of Africa, but not the entire continent.

Travel advisories are issued periodically to cover countries considered as risky to travel to by anyone who has to go there for any reason. Sudan, Democratic Republic of the Congo, Libya and Somalia have been included in past lists issued by the authorities involved. Security concerns in Africa, as in other parts of the world, may change rapidly. It's a good idea to check the U.S. Department of State website for more information about travel warnings and Africa and the countries involved.

HEALTH RELATED CONCERNS IN AFRICAN COUNTRIES

Other concerns may be health related. Will they be safe from the various diseases that are known to be rampant on the continent? Will they be safe from Ebola? Will they be safe from malaria?

Again, these are legitimate concerns to have where Africa is concerned, particularly if it involves traveling there for any reason. After all, Ebola and malaria are real and have caused great havoc in certain parts of Africa over the years. It wasn't too long ago when the world became fixated on the Ebola epidemic in West Africa as a result of the intense media hype and publicity it received in the global media. Like the rest of the horror stories about Africa, the global media reported extensively on the outbreak of the deadly disease that had no cure, killed people infected within days and did so in a terrifying manner. People still recoil in horror at the mere mention of Ebola. The pictures of the dead and dying are seared into the memories of those who saw them on television and in the newspapers. But is Ebola a threat to everyone who travels to Africa? The answer is no. It has been detected only in certain areas of the continent. Additionally, all outbreaks of the disease receive intense media publicity. The global media makes sure the world knows all about Ebola outbreaks in terms of the area, the scope and everything else people need to know about it.

MALARIA

Malaria is a serious and sometimes fatal tropical disease spread by mosquitoes and other parasites. Malaria parasites breed in warmer climates where there is a lot of rain and humidity and is more common in countries with warm, humid weather. It is a risk to travelers visiting many African countries the majority of which are located in the tropical zone. However, it is completely preventable if certain precautionary measures are taken. They include taking malaria prevention tablets prior and while traveling, avoiding mosquito bites by wearing mosquito netting and spraying whenever possible.

HIV-AIDS

HIV is a virus that attacks cells in the immune system, which is the body's natural defense against illness.

HIV stands for human immunodeficiency virus. It is the virus that can lead to acquired immunodeficiency syndrome, or AIDS, if not treated.

AIDS is generally described as a set of symptoms and illnesses that develop as a result of advanced HIV infection which has destroyed the immune system.

Africa is reported to have the worst record of HIV AIDS infection. Here again, media hype has resulted in publicizing the notion that Africa has the most cases of HIV AIDS cases in the world since its outbreak, claiming thousands of victims. Essentially, it is a global health issue that seems to have been contained, at least it is not as much a threat as before. Again, it lies within reason to know what it's all about.

How does one prevent oneself from becoming a victim of malaria or any of the other deadly infectious diseases known to be rampant in Africa?

The general rule in most countries is that people traveling to foreign countries take a number of precautions that are medical in nature. These include vaccinations against malaria in the case of Africa and other tropical regions. Usually, those measures prevail, if adhered to.

HEALTH SAFETY

It lies within reason to consider doing what most people do when they decide to travel to another country, by making sure they know the health risks involved. Africa is no different. In fact, Africa might very well give people more reason to be concerned given the kind of hype and publicity the continent has gotten lately about the outbreak of deadly diseases such as Ebola and other infectious diseases. Updates are available on many government and non-government websites about vaccines for diseases that are common throughout the African continent. Hepatitis A and B, typhoid, yellow fever and rabies are some of the more common diseases that are mentioned. Safety should also be a consideration when choosing food and drinks. Buying from roadside vendors, very common in most African countries can be considered to be risky.

CHAPTER FOUR

WHY AFRICAN AMERICANS AND PEOPLE OF AFRICAN DESCENT AROUND THE GLOBE 'GO BACK' TO AFRICA

Many African Americans and others of African lineage from different parts of the globe travel to Africa for various reasons that may include business, tourism and travel vacation to another continent just to get away from their home surroundings. Lately, an entirely new and perhaps a more compelling and meaningful reason to travel to Africa is rapidly increasing in popularity. They are going back to Africa, their ancestral home. And that is all that matters, as far as they are concerned. Their destination is a continent they call the 'Motherland'. It is an extraordinary journey that has become immensely significant, particularly to those who begin to consider Africa as more than the continent of their heritage, those who look at Africa as the continent they want to return to live for the rest of their lives.

Recent reports in different media have focused on the trend and have described it as having the characteristics of an exodus by African-Americans from the United States to Africa. For many in black communities in America and other parts of the world these days, going back to Africa has become nothing short of a necessary component of a life's journey, worth making every effort possible to fulfill.

For many African-Americans traveling to Africa has become as significant as a pilgrimage. Interestingly enough, the renewed interest in Africa and increase in the number of African-Americans traveling to Africa has contributed to the emergence of the concept of 2019 as the YEAR OF RETURN. The central theme of the yearlong celebrations is the declaration to people of African descent all over the world to consider Africa as the ancestral home to which they are entitled to return to visit for vacation or business purposes or to repatriate to and live on a permanent basis.

MANY AFRICAN AMERICANS AND OTHERS OF AFRICAN LINEAGE FROM OTHER PARTS OF THE WORLD TRAVEL TO AFRICA FOR BUSINESS AND JOBS

It is also true that other African Americans travel to Africa purely for business reasons. Their motivation derives from the same values that have driven business people of all races and nationalities who travel to Africa for business: they are looking for opportunities to invest, maximize their profits and find new markets for products. They may be in business for themselves or may be employed by one of the transnational companies that have offices all over the world. Traveling to Africa for such an individual might be part of the responsibilities of the position they hold, which means all expenses may be paid for by the company or nonprofit organization that employs him or her. In other words, many African American entrepreneurs travel to Africa on business trips undertaken for the purpose of doing business, with nothing else in mind.

OTHER AFRICAN AMERICANS TRAVEL TO AFRICA JUST FOR FUN

There is another category of visitors from African American communities that travel to Africa. Quite a few take the trip as part of a tour package and chose Africa because they can afford it, not necessarily because they want to reconnect with the people and the continent from which their ancestors originated. They go to Africa in search of the thrills and excitement associated with visiting and touring tropical and exotic countries and look for nothing but the fun of it. Going to Africa for such individuals is not considered on any other merits other than what it offers by way of interesting places to visit, best restaurants to dine, great hotels and places to shop so they can bring back gifts to family and friends.

REASONS WHY MANY AFRICAN AMERICANS AND OTHERS FROM THE DIASPORA ARE GOING BACK TO AFRICA

By the same token, increasing numbers of African Americans and others of African lineage from around the globe have embraced the notion that repatriating to Africa is a far better option than continuing to live in countries in North America, the Caribbean and Europe where they are made to feel like second class citizens and subjected to acts of brutality perpetrated by police and law enforcement authorities. They are aware of the danger that looms over black people in a country like America where they can get killed for no reason other than being at the wrong place at the wrong time, the only reason the police need to use deadly force to shoot to kill African Americans.

For many African Americans today, repatriating to Africa provides the opportunity to make a bold statement: they prefer the dignity of living in an environment in which they don't have to deal with racial bias and bigotry of the white power structure. Being part of the movement of returning to Africa essentially means proclaiming to the world that they have taken the final and ultimate step of redemption; they are going back to the land of their ancestors. Unlike immigrants from Africa who immigrate to America and Europe and elsewhere, returning or repatriating to Africa by African-Americans and others of African lineage from around the globe is not just a change of environment to explore the potential of setting up a business or pursuing a career. Many make the move with the feeling that they are going back 'home' to countries in Africa where they plan to live for the rest of their lives. They have, for all intents and purposes, made Africa their new home and expect to settle there and begin a new life. It is a unique homecoming for people of African descent in the African diaspora, considered by most as the ultimate act of spiritual and cultural rebirth.

HOW TO PREPARE TO GO TO AFRICA BEGINNING WITH CHOOSING AN AFRICAN COUNTRY

One of the challenges is the country to go to in Africa. And the question becomes: which country in Africa is best for those seeking to be exposed to the real life in Africa for the tourist and which one would gratify the quest to 'reconnect' with their heritage, for others with plans to repatriate and make a new home in Africa.

Expectations differ, depending on the reasons for going to Africa. For those for whom Africa is just another continent to visit or go on a safari to explore the "exotic' jungle life there is plenty of adventure and excitement in tour packages that deliver precisely what they are looking for.

To those repatriating, it is a journey with a purpose and has to be undertaken with the goal of fulfilling the mission that is taking them to the African continent. It is a whole new ballgame with the latter.

DEALING WITH THE BASICS

In many ways, going to Africa is not much different from going anywhere else. It's pretty much the same in terms of what is involved when it comes to intercontinental travel. The basics remain unchanged, regardless of which country in Africa is the destination. Securing passports, applying for visas, getting inoculations are all routine. The routine stuff usually involves a trip downtown to the post office or the county office building to get passport forms or inquire about vaccinations and other things related to what one needs to do to be able to travel outside the borders of the country. Doing these things means you are simply doing what everyone is supposed to do. They are the rules and regulations all must abide by when it comes to traveling from one country or continent to another.

The question is: does one have to prepare in any special kind of way when Africa is the destination? Does one have to do anything else besides the routine stuff that everyone does when traveling overseas?

This is where it gets tricky and complicated in part because a lot of factors come into play. Basically it involves preparing in such a way that the trip will go smoothly, allow you to fully reap all the benefits and accomplish the objective that sent you there. And it all begins with one question: which African country to go to.

FACTORS TO CONSIDER WHEN CHOOSING AN AFRICAN COUNTRY TO VISIT. TO DO BUSINESS OR REPATRIATE TO

It is indeed a huge challenge for those repatriating to find a country to go to in Africa that will make it possible to gratify the quest to 'reconnect' with their heritage.

Many African Americans have made mistakes in the process that could have been avoided if they had asked the right questions from the right sources. Verna Davis of Syracuse, NY, comes to mind. A couple of fundamental errors on her part set her up to face challenges she was not prepared for and didn't know how to deal with and made her trip to Africa nothing short of a nightmare.

BEST TO CHOOSE AN ENGLISH SPEAKING AFRICAN COUNTRY IF YOU KNOW AND SPEAK ONLY ENGLISH

She boarded a plane for the Ivory Coast in West Africa and had no idea what lay ahead of her, until she set foot in the country and found out that she had gone to the wrong place. The common language was French. She had no knowledge of French. And that set the stage for all the problems that followed. Attempts to communicate with sign language didn't work. They couldn't understand her, no matter how hard she tried. Frustrated, confused, alarmed and disappointed, she decided to leave the Ivory Coast.

What had been planned as a happy reunion with her people turned into a nightmare. A call to an African friend back in the United States led to arrangements being made for her to continue her trip to Ghana where English is the common language. She returned to America without the kind of fond memories most people bring with them when they visit places of historical significance to them, particularly if it has to do with their heritage.

WAYS TO REAP ALL THE BENEFITS OF TRAVELING TO AFRICA

So what's the best approach when it comes to getting the most from a trip to Africa? A lot is involved in the process but the decision made regarding the nature of the trip pretty much determines how to prepare for it. Those repatriating have a lot more to deal with than those just visiting. Regardless, getting realistic information is the key to being able to prepare adequately. The sources for information about Africa are plentiful. Most of the sources are easily accessible and include the usual places we all go to these days in search for information: the world wide web. The African continent is widely covered on the internet. Chose a country where communication won't be a problem. For most Americans, any country in Anglophile Africa is a far better option. In those countries, English is the dominant language. Ability to speak and write French is ideal in an African country such as Benin or Togoland where French is the common language.

CHAPTER FIVE

AFRICAN AMERICAN INFLUENCE IN AFRICA MOST DIASPORA AFRICANS DON'T KNOW ABOUT

The majority of African Americans have no idea about the degree to which hip hop culture has influenced contemporary culture and the general lifestyle of the people in other countries, particularly Africa. In the context of this discussion, by hip hop culture, we are referring to the music, fashion, entertainment and lifestyle that originated in America among the younger generation decades ago and is now a major component of American contemporary culture. African Americans are credited with playing a major role in its creation. And it has made a huge impact in Africa. So pervasive is the influence of the hip-hop culture that practically every aspect of contemporary culture in most African countries has been affected.

Evidence of the impact is all too obvious. In the streets in most African countries, men and women take particular pride in wearing the kind of clothing described in the media as urban gear, bearing fashion labels and trademarks that are the creations of African Americans in the hip hop apparel industry.

The music played on radio stations and popular entertainment places tend to be rhythm and blues by leading African American artists or the local version of hip hop which is basically a fusion of American rhythm and blues and African vocals with the characteristic up-tempo beat. TV stations air programs featuring African American movies and reality shows. African American owned television programming has a huge fan base in Africa and is favored by a considerable portion of the television viewing audience in most African countries.

THE AFRICAN AMERICAN 'COOL' AND HIP HOP LIFESTYLE AND CULTURE HAVE PROFOUNDLY IMPACTED CONTEMPORARY AFRICAN CULTURE

To most Africans, the American 'cool' is best represented by African Americans in ways that are unique to African Americans and in a fashion that only African Americans have mastered.

No matter what it is, to most Africans, particularly the youth and young adults, the African American 'cool' is the true representation of cultural trends in America. It ranges from the street lingo to the latest dance steps to the current jewelry sported by African American celebrities.

Problem is: the average African American doesn't know about the impact contemporary African American culture, often referred to as hiphop, has on their African counterparts in the continent most refer to fondly as the 'motherland' Africa.

AFRICAN CULTURES HAVE ALSO INFLUENCED CONTEMPORARY CULTURAL TRENDS IN AMERICA AND ELSEWHERE

Facebook and other social media appear to have played a significant role in publicizing the emergence of a new phenomenon within the African-American-American community. The new cultural phenomenon is characterized by people with names such as Funali Yira, Imam Abdul Aziz, Queenrighteoulsyrefined, Nubian Queen, Earthly Expressions, Ebonynubia, Akua Agusi, Akua Gray, Empressima Ethiopia, Empress Nubia, Khalid Bey.

Anyone who is familiar with African names will recognize a few of them are West African. Akua is a popular name in Ghana. The Akan tribe which consists of the Fantis, Ashantis, the Akwapims, the Twis and others give most females born on Wednesdays that name at birth. Other names have more of the ancient Egyptian, Ethiopian flavor.

To others, the names may sound strange or exotic. But to them, it is a conscious and deliberate attempt to identify themselves by names that indicate an intent on their part to portray a connection with other cultures, particularly African, using the age old model that begins with names that have significance in terms of stating who they are, what they stand for, and where they are going.

They say and do things that reflect a conscious commitment to living a lifestyle which Western culture would describe as holistic or spiritual, or naturalists would describe as close to nature. They practice and encourage others to farm and grow their own food as part of the process of staying away from processed foods. They wear outfits that have a distinct ethnic African oriented flavor and talk about a lifestyle that is different from the norm in America today and more often than not, they are based on traditional African culture. They have succeeded in giving a new dimension to the concept of Black Beauty by Africanizing it. And they have done so by glamorizing African hairstyles, native traditional costumes, even footwear in ways that conventional fashion could not do. Most importantly, the majority don't shy away from openly expressing a desire to go to Africa, to explore the possibility of repatriating. Such trends have contributed to the increasing interest in Africa among African Americans and others of African descent around the world.

CHAPTER SIX

LIFE IN AFRICA FOR AFRICAN AMERICANS

Faced with the challenge of coping with life in an environment in which the culture and lifestyle are completely different from what they had known in their communities in terms of the music, fashion, food and almost everything else, African Americans who travel to Africa, especially those who have decided to repatriate, have to deal with a completely different reality; living in two worlds simultaneously. One is city life in urban areas in Africa, characterized by the modern lifestyle that has been greatly influenced by American and European cultures.

African Americans and others of African descent from other parts of the world may not encounter any serious problems with the modern Africa in part because certain aspects may be familiar. Nightclubs, restaurants, hotels and other places of entertainment almost always have an European or American identity of sorts and make every effort to appeal to those with a mostly foreign cultural sensibility. The other is the traditional and old African lifestyle that tends to be totally foreign to those not born and raised in Africa.

Embracing a new lifestyle as they pursue whatever interests they may have, raising their children, finding and holding jobs and trying to live normal lives in such an environment is not easy and has the potential to develop into something not dissimilar to a cross cultural conflict that pits the old against the new, Western culture against traditional African values, and the question becomes: how does one not born and raised in Africa navigate the cultural terrain?

THE NEW AND THE OLD AFRICA

Again, the uniqueness of Africa derives from its duality: the old and the new. There is a new, modern and urbanized side of Africa that is not too different from what one sees in urban settings around the globe. Its major characteristics are high rise apartments, skyscraper office buildings, wide expressways with SUV sport utility vehicles driven by men and women wearing all kinds of urban gear, with their smartphones, stylish haircuts and elegant hairstyles. This is the part of Africa people see on television and social media these days. It is that side of modern Africa that strives to be a part of the global marketplace with cities, airports, airlines and infrastructure that connect them with other parts of the world, where people access the Internet and chat with others around the globe. The lifestyle in this part of modern Africa has as its most striking characteristic, a close resemblance to what exists in most urban and metropolitan areas in America or in Europe.

Here the pace of life is determined by forces that are in play in similar settings around the globe, where modern life manifests itself in diverse ways. This is the lifestyle that has turned a number of African cities such as Lagos in Nigeria, Accra in Ghana, and Johannesburg in South Africa into notoriously dangerous places in which no one's safety is guaranteed. This is the part of Africa where tourists are warned to be careful and to watch every move they make. These are the urbanized areas where crime is rampant, hustlers abound and prey on innocent victims, making downtown Lagos, Nigeria or Accra, Ghana, just as dangerous as it is in New York or Chicago, if not more.

THE OLD AND TRADITIONAL ASPECT OF THE AFRICAN LIFESTYLE HAS ITS ADVANTAGES AND DISADVANTAGES: FOUND MOSTLY IN RURAL AREAS

As for the other face of Africa, it is pristine, idyllic, mysterious, where the past is very much a part of the present. The people here seem to prefer to live in a world relatively untouched by the rapid advances of the modern technological and digital age. These are the small communities of villages and towns where the people have retained most of the traditional beliefs that govern their way of life. In such small communities, the impact of modernization has been minimal, and has not done much to influence the local population in terms of cultivating patterns of behavior usually found in urban areas. Their approach to life is rooted in their culture, their understanding of and relationship to nature and the forces that are assumed to have the power and ability to influence their lives. Their lifestyle is based on centuries old way of life and a culture that inculcates into them early in life a sense of what life in that environment is all about. They have embraced cultures and lifestyles that have evolved their own ways of punishing those whose actions can be perceived as wrong, as well as rewarding those who do the right thing. These are cultures in which, not too long ago, anyone caught stealing could be punished by having an arm cut off, so there wouldn't be an arm to use to steal anymore, and proved to be quite effective in deterring others from stealing.

CULTURAL CHALLENGES

The cultural landscape in Africa is not easy to navigate, especially for those not born and raised there. It is a continent of many languages, cultures, ethnicities and lifestyles. The old world of ancient monuments and traditions coexist with modern cities with new lifestyles and cultural influences that have been imported into Africa over the years as a result of their interactions with people from other parts of the world, especially Europe and America.

American and European influence is evident in many ways, but the cultural landscape is dominated by traditions, customs and norms that are peculiar to tribes and communities and are not easy to understand and or relate to by others not born and raised in those communities or who don't belong to the tribes in question.

HOW TO NAVIGATE THE CULTURAL LANDSCAPE IN AFRICA: IMPORTANT TO KNOW THAT THERE IS NO ONE AFRICAN CULTURE

A common misconception about Africa is that it is a continent with one culture, which suggests that all Africans share the same culture and everything else associated with it. It is a total misrepresentation of the African continent, its culture and its people by others from different continents with little or no knowledge about the reality of life in Africa. To the contrary, Africa is one of the most diverse continents in terms of its ethnic composition and cultural diversity. The entire continent is populated by tribal groups with cultures that may differ significantly enough from each other to be perceived as not being similar.

DEALING WITH GOVERNMENT BUREAUCRACY. AFRICAN PUNCTUALITY. BLACK PEOPLE'S TIME

A source of frustration to most Europeans and Americans when interacting with Africans is what they might see as a seemingly lack of effort on the part of Africans to act in ways that reflect a conscious and concerted attempt to do things in a strictly timely fashion. While most Americans and Europeans are known to approach all situations with the aim of being punctual and on time, Africans tend to be more inclined to follow their own notion of African punctuality. It basically means people take their time to do things creating situations where things don't get done on time. This is not to suggest that nothing gets done on time.

CHAPTER SEVEN

RELOCATING TO AFRICA BY AFRICAN AMERICANS AND OTHERS OF AFRICAN DESCENT: FULL OF CHALLENGES BUT EXCITING AND FULFILLING FOR THOSE WHO REPATRIATE

Marcus Garvey made returning to Africa one of the major themes of a campaign he launched in the early twentieth century. His goal was to organize people of African descent in North America and elsewhere to relocate to Africa. The rationale was simple; Africa would welcome and provide them with the freedom denied them in other countries. Returning to Africa would mean going back home to the land of their ancestry, away from the racism, prejudice and bias perpetrated against people of African descent in America and Europe. It was referred to as the Back to Africa movement.

He made a huge impact with his message and succeeded in setting in motion a movement for freedom that served as a catalyst for the civil rights movements. The 'BACK TO Africa' movement continues today. Over the years, many African-Americans have relocated to different countries in Africa, appear to have made a smooth transition and have succeeded in adapting to the new lifestyle.

SUCCESSFUL STORIES OF AFRICAN AMERICANS WHO HAVE REPATRIATED TO AFRICA

Imahkus Njinga Okofu Ababio from New York City chose Ghana as the country to repatriate to several years ago. Entrepreneurial and business savvy, she decided to go into business and created a beach resort on the Atlantic coast at a location not too far from the infamous castle in Ghana where the majority of African slaves were kept before they were shipped across the Atlantic Ocean. Today, the resort is a favorite hangout for African Americans, Africans and other tourists to Ghana. On her FACEBOOK page are pictures of a beautiful seaside resort in the kind of tropical setting unique to Africa, including a picture with a former President of Ghana.

Imahkhus is not alone. All indications are that she feels at home in her new environment and has been embraced by the community in which she lives. She appears to have made a successful transition from life in America, settled down in a community that provides her with the opportunity to begin a new life in a totally different environment. She is definitely a success story and an example for others to follow. Similar stories of African Americans relocating to African countries and setting up successful businesses, engaging with the people in different ways and becoming active participants' in community life have been widely reported in the media.

JEROME THOMPSON. MARYLAND NATIVE IS HAPPILY RETIRED IN GHANA

Jerome Thompson, formerly of Maryland made the decision to retire to Ghana and built his house in Prampram, a fishing community on the Atlantic coast. His ocean front house is located close to the seashore, giving him the luxury of easy access to the beach. He has said in several interviews with different media that he has found the ideal location to enjoy his retirement and has no regrets for making the decision to repatriate to Ghana. He has lived in Ghana for more than ten years.

He is one of many African-Americans and others of African descent from the diaspora who made the decision to relocate to Africa because they see the potential to bring real change to their lives. With professional degrees and skills that have not gotten them the kind of jobs or the upward mobility they seek, they see a fresh start in a new setting in an African country as a better option. Others just want to enjoy their retirement in a peaceful environment, away from the hustle and bustle of America and other countries. Most importantly, they seek to live in an environment in which they don't have to deal with racism and prejudice that have been perpetrated against people of African descent in America and Europe.

5000 AFRICAN AMERICANS LIVE IN ACCRA, GHANA'S CAPITAL; GROWING POPULATIONS OF AFRICAN AMERICANS IN OTHER AFRICAN COUNTRIES

According to 2014 estimates, more than 5000 African Americans and people of Caribbean descent live in Accra, the capital of Ghana, a country of about 30 million people.

While some returnees have gone through the emotional journey of tracing their families through DNA testing, for the majority who just go to visit, or to settle like Jeremy Thompson, the feeling of being "home" on the continent is the ultimate satisfaction.

Today, African Americans and others of African descent who have relocated to Africa can be seen in many African countries. Many prefer the urban setting of African cities and find jobs in professional positions with various organizations. The more adventurous ones go out into the rural communities in the hinterland where they engage in farming, and produce food for themselves and the communities in which they live. Majority make a smooth transition and appear to succeed in dealing with the challenges that such a change in lifestyle usually brings.

CHAPTER EIGHT

WHY GHANA HAS EMERGED AS THE FAVORITE AFRICAN COUNTRY FOR AFRICAN AMERICAN RETURNEES AND OTHERS FROM THE AFRICAN DIASPORA

In spite of the bad press that the African continent gets from the global media, recent reports from the International Monetary Fund and other organizations and experts who have analyzed trends in Africa appear to paint a different picture. The consensus is that Africa is not all doom and gloom. In a recent report, the African Development Bank revealed that Africa is the world's second-fastest growing economy, and has provided data and information to support the notion that Africa is not in as bad a shape as many have been led to believe by the global media.

The economies of many African countries have been on the upswing and appear to be positioned to sustain their growth and expansion in the future. Ghana, for example, has been cited for its political stability, steady economic growth, consistent progress and the eagerness of the government to embrace change and new ideas. The first African country south of the Sahara Desert to achieve independence from the British in 1957, Ghana has taken center stage as one of the few countries in Africa with a thriving economy, a stable government actually practicing a democratic form of governance, an effective financial infrastructure and a population that is actively involved in the political process and exercises the power of the vote in elections.

GHANA IS A DEMOCRACRATIC COUNTRY. A GROWING ECONOMY. STABLE SOCIAL AND POLITICAL INSTITUTIONS AND A SAFE COUNTRY TO TRAVEL TO

Tourists from all over the world are flocking to Ghana. Foreign investments in the country have increased dramatically. Freedom of speech and the press is evidenced by a sharp increase in the number of radio stations, newspapers, and television stations that promote public and open discussion of issues. In an interview broadcast on BBC, a former head of state, President Kuffour said Ghana currently has more than 200 radio stations. Most importantly, the government and its leaders have proclaimed their dedication to, respect for and adherence to the ideals of democracy, and available evidence suggests that there has been an effort to sustain a democratic form of government over the past several decades. There is an elected parliament with members representing various districts and a president who is elected every four years.

It comes as no surprise that the majority of African Americans and others of African descent from Europe and other parts of the globe seem to focus on Ghana. It has become the country of choice for those planning to travel to Africa to explore the potential of repatriating there as well as those who have already made the move, have repatriated and have joined the growing number of 'returnees'. It makes sense to choose to go to a country that appears to have attained a reasonably decent level of social, economic and political development in addition to the historically significant notion of being the first African country to become independent from colonialism.

THERE IS POLITICAL STABILITY AND SOLID EVIDENCE OF PROGRESS IN OTHER PARTS OF AFRICA

South Africa has been transformed within the past two decades from an apartheid state into a parliamentary democracy where the fundamental elements of a democratic government seem to be in play. So are Liberia, Sierra Leone, Uganda, Zambia, Senegal and others in both Francophone and Anglophone Africa. Sierra and Liberia survived civil wars.

GHANA TAKES THE INITIATIVE WITH 'YEAR OF RETURN' LAUNCH. GOVERNMENT INVITES AFRICAN AMERICANS. JAMAICANS AND DIASPORAN AFRICANS TO VISIT AND REPATRIATE TO GHANA AND OTHER AFRICAN COUNTRIES

In September 2018, President Akufo Addo of Ghana declared in a speech in Washington DC that the Ghana government has committed to a policy initiative dedicated to making it easier for African Americans and others of African descent from the diaspora to return to Ghana. The occasion marked the launch what is now referred to as the "Year of Return". That was precisely what many African Americans, West Indians in the Caribbean and others of African lineage around the world had been waiting for. They had long sought for some form of action from African governments that would encourage, recognize and support those who want to repatriate to Africa. For years, they have articulated the need for

African governments to be more sensitive to their concerns and complaints about the difficulties they face in their efforts to return to Africa, especially with issues dealing with the rights of residency. Reaction from the African American communities to the Ghana led 'Year of Return' initiative was one of relief and elation, especially for those who were thinking about repatriating to Africa.

The 'Year of Return' initiative is perceived as the answer to most of the questions that have been raised over the years.

The fact that the initiative was made by the Ghana government gave it more weight. Ghana was one of the main points of departure for the slave ships. One such point of departure is a huge castle that was built in 1492 and has become a leading tourist attraction for African diasporans who go to Ghana.

CHAPTER NINE

TWO NEW YORKERS PLANNING TO TRAVEL.
REPATRIATE TO AFRICA: DIFFERENT
BACKGROUNDS. DIFFERENT PERSPECTIVES
BUT SEEKING THE SAME GOAL: RETURNING
TO THEIR ANCESTRAL HOMELAND

What lies ahead for African Americans or others from the African diaspora who travel to Africa as returnees who have repatriated? How different is the experience for those visiting Africa for a short period as opposed to those who are repatriating and plan to assume permanent residence and live there for the rest of their lives?

Meet two individuals from the African diaspora who have made the decision to go back to Africa. As part of the research into the writing of this book, we focused on the life experiences of two individuals who are in the process of realizing a lifelong aspiration to 'go back' to Africa.

One is an African American, born and raised in America. He wants to go to Africa primarily because it has been one of his lifelong aspirations, and believes that the trip to Africa will provide him with a sense of fulfilment. The other individual is a Jamaican who has lived most of his life in America. He has already made up his mind to repatriate to an African country and has chosen Ghana as the country where he would begin his quest for a new home in Africa.

Both based the decision to travel to Africa on their understanding of the significance of their ancestral linkage to the African continent and are convinced that their life experiences have prepared and provided them with the knowledge and insight they need to make the transition from life in America to life in Africa.

HE CONSIDERS HIMSELF A TYPICAL AFRICAN AMERICAN FROM THE HOOD

Peter Wynn is his name. He is in his late fifties and says going to Africa will fulfill a lifelong aspiration to return to the land of his ancestry. Born and raised in Syracuse, New York, his life experiences have exposed him to various lifestyles and cultures in America and the Caribbean and played a significant role in his decision to go to Africa.

INNER CITY NEIGHBORHOODS TYPICALLY DON'T TEACH PRIDE IN AFRICA

According to Wynn, he grew up in an environment dominated by the hood culture. Typical of inner city America, the neighborhood in which he grew up in Syracuse had no connection whatsoever with Africa and did nothing to encourage him to relate to Africa in any positive manner. Identifying with Africa was not on anyone's agenda. It didn't happen in school or at home. Pride in Africa was not high on the priorities of people in the world in which he grew up back in the day. It is a world that only black people can relate to in part because it is populated mostly by black people. It's typical inner city America, often described as the hood and a world only black people can understand and relate to that has its own language, music, fashion, food and culinary traditions, even its own peculiar codes of conduct that teach them early how to survive in a world dominated by the white power structure.

His education followed the pattern that had been criticized for miseducating rather than educating black youth, a system that makes no effort to encourage the youth to relate to Africa in a positive manner. Most of the information he gathered about Africa came from his interest in reading and research into subjects that included Africa. Later as an adult, his interaction with Africans at work and in the streets gave him the chance to learn and gather more information and data about Africa and Africans.

According to Wynn, the media had the same effect on him over the years as another source of misinformation and miseducation about Africa and Africans. Television networks, print media newspapers and magazines published news items, articles and editorials that made him look at Africa and Africans as representing something not to be proud of. Portrayed in the worst possible light, Africans were described in the media as primitive, living in huts and trees, poor and disease ridden and totally out of touch with the rest of the world. Like most of his peers, he found himself with feelings about Africa and Africans that were a mixture of ambivalence and confusion, a state of mind characteristic of the majority of African American men who grow up in inner cities in America. With no access to the correct information and data, most end up with little or no knowledge of Africa, certainly not in a way that would make them feel proud of the fact that their ancestors are from Africa. He realized the truth when he stepped out into the world and began to deal with the reality of life for a black man in America.

ENCOUNTERS WITH THE CRIMINAL JUSTICE SYSTEM REVEALS RACIAL INEQUALITY AND PREJUDICE IN AMERICAN SOCIETY

His encounters with the criminal justice system exposed him to some of the harsh realities for life for black people in America. Like most of his peers, he found himself caught up in a criminal justice system with a police force that seemed to have the power and authority to make his life miserable whenever they decided to do so. More importantly, he became aware of the disparities that exist in American society when it comes to the rights and privileges of black people, the potential for innocent black people to become victims of a criminal justice system that makes no secret of its bias and prejudice against them. He came to grips with the fact that black communities in America have been made powerless and exploited by the system, had been denied their rights and had effectively become second class citizens in a country that prides itself on promoting human rights. He came to the conclusion that it is a system that has been set up to deny Black people access to jobs, housing, educational opportunities and financial resources.

AWARENESS LEADS TO ASKING QUESTIONS

Awareness of the disparities in the criminal justice system, unemployment in the black communities, discrimination and bias in housing, criminal justice system, education, financing and the provision of health services led him to ask the question; why? The all too obvious answer was: racism and prejudice in America. The beneficiaries of white privilege in America have created a system that makes it possible for the white power structure to have more access to the rights and privileges that all citizens are entitled to as a constitutional right guaranteed by law. They also have the resources to continue to do things that weaken the black community and the ability to use systemic ways such as those used by law enforcement to entrap and imprison black people for committing crimes that people of other races get less time for.

Peter Wynn credits two trips that gave him more insights into life in America for white and black Americans. In Provincetown, New England, and later in the Caribbean island of St Thomas, he was exposed to different cultures and learned how to live in communities in which the dominant culture and the lifestyle of the people differed from what he was used to.

AFRICA IS THE MOTHERLAND. THAT'S WHY I WANT TO GO THERE. SAYS PETER WYNN

Over the years, he had been made aware that his heritage is African, yet the history books and media provided information and data that didn't clarify things for him to really understand and appreciate his African heritage. He had to deal with a system that appeared to focus on making sure he had no access to the relevant information that would help him to relate to his heritage in a meaningful manner. He knows better now, and has no problem showing pride in his African heritage. According to Wynn, making the decision to travel to Africa reflects his understanding and acceptance of the fact that Africa is the continent of his ancestry.

READY AND PREPARED TO COPE WITH THE CHALLENGES AND PROBLEMS OF LIVING IN AFRICA AS AN AFRICAN AMERICAN

He knows he is prepared to cope with the challenges he would face as a New Yorker in Africa. It would come as no surprise to him, if they expect him to know little or nothing about African history and culture, find fault with the food, and act with typical American naiveté and ignorance of Africa and Africans. He would prove them wrong and show them how well he had prepared over the years for his trip to Africa. His experience in the Caribbean had taught him quite a few things about life in a culture that is totally different from American culture, how to assimilate and learn from people in order to be able to interact with them. They have no idea that he has accumulated a vast knowledge of African history, culture, politics, food and cuisines and knows a few phrases of a couple of African languages. As far as Wynn is concerned, he is ready to go to Africa.

HE IS ON A MISSION TO SAVE AFRICA

His name is Ras Lawrence and he is on a mission: he is repatriating to Africa to bring change to the continent. Ras Lawrence looks at Africa from the perspective of a Jamaican who has lived in America and sees limitless potential for growth and development for the African continent. As far as he is concerned, African countries have all the resources needed to develop the various sectors of their economies and become independent in reality. Africans lag behind the rest of the world because they have been victimized and exploited by Europeans and Americans who have used various strategies to gain control of their resources, exposed them to cultures, ideologies, religions and educational systems that are totally foreign to them and are in conflict with everything they know.

According to him, that kind of insight and perspective into the plight of Africa can only be developed by people like him who have experienced life in Western countries, and have been exposed to both the best and worst of both worlds. People like him with such a background don't feel intimidated by the white power structure because they have lived in it, survived and thrived in spite of all the obstacles they have to deal with and have a better understanding of the situation as it relates to the overall strategy of the white power structure towards Africa and people of African descent. The mindset he has developed over the years qualifies him to speak on behalf of Africa and Africans who seem to be afraid to confront the truth about their situation.

He credits his unique perspective with providing him with the foresight and courage to formulate grand visions of launching businesses, building financial infrastructures and starting social programs and cultural activities all aimed at accomplishing one objective: create sustainable economies in Africa that will free Africa and Africans from depending on America and Europe.

HE HAS PLANS TO BUILD INFRASTRUCTURE. CREATE SOCIAL AND CULTURAL PROGRAMS AND FINANCIAL NETWORKS TO MAINTAIN SUSTAINABLE ECONOMIES AND MAKE AFRICA SELF SUFFICIENT

He envisages playing a leading role in an elaborate and comprehensive plan that would create the conditions and the environment in which Africa and Africans would live in peace and harmony with each other. As far as he is concerned, Africa has all the resources it needs to make it a dominant force in the global marketplace. That can happen with a change of mindset on the part of both the African leaders and the general population. His plan of action for Africa aims at ending exploitation of Africa by foreign powers, especially America and Europe. Exploitation of Africa by Europe and America has to stop. Africans have to begin to take pride in their heritage and history, and resolve to develop their countries in ways that benefit the entire populations, not just a few. He blames all the confusion, political instability, underdeveloped economies, corruption and mismanagement on outside forces who found ways to exploit Africa and Africans for centuries. The exploitation will not cease if a radical and revolutionary approach is not used as part of the strategy.

Returning to Africa is more than a return to the land of his ancestry. It is a journey that began when he left Jamaica as a youngster. Kept alive and nurtured over the years, his aspiration to go to Africa is finally being fulfilled. He has made the decision to go back to a world where he can make an impact and contribute to the development of the African continent in a pragmatic manner. According to Ras, he refuses to be trapped in a culture that has justified slavery in the past and continues to use other ways to maintain supremacy of one race over another. He prefers to identify with his African heritage now in everything he does. To him, African culture is rich, unique and magnificent and should be embraced as part of the overall process of reconnecting with Africa.

GOING BACK TO AFRICA IS THE BEGINNING OF A NEW PHASE IN LIFE FOR RAS LAWRENCE

Repatriating to Africa will be the beginning of a new phase in his life dedicated to bringing real change to Africa. Just talking about it is not enough. It is time for concrete action geared towards pursuing sustainable goals that will create change in Africa.

It is common knowledge, he says, that Africa has the potential to become self-sufficient in all areas of life. No continent has more arable land for farming than Africa, yet the majority of African countries are not able to feed their people and have to import food. That is a crying shame and must change. African countries have the professional expertise, knowledge and experience to build factories and other infrastructure to manufacture various products for the entire continent. All the gold, diamonds, bauxite, aluminum, oil and mining industries in Africa have to be controlled by Africans, not Europeans and American conglomerates whose main goal is to maximize andretrieve their profits. They are not particularly interested in the economic and social development of the African countries in which they operate. He advocates for change in all aspects as part of the goal to make Africa less dependent on outside sources. Africans have to develop the mindset that they can take care of themselves, have no need to depend on Europe or America for help, and take pride in their ability to provide for themselves.

According to him, returnees from America and elsewhere around the globe will play an important role in the development of the various African countries they chose to repatriate to begin a new life. Their expertise in various areas such as technology, engineering and finance will make it possible for them to contribute to the development goals of the African continent as a whole.

CHAPTER TEN

DO AFRICAN PEOPLE AND GOVERNMENTS WELCOME AFRICAN AMERICANS AND OTHERS OF AFRICAN DESCENT WHO VISIT OR REPATRIATE TO AFRICA?

How do Africans on the continent relate to African-Americans and others of African descent who are born and raised in other cultures? Do African governments and the people embrace and welcome African Americans and people of African descent from the diaspora who visit or repatriate to Africa?

Africans in general appear to have no problem relating to their counterparts from America, the West Indies or any part of the world for that matter. There is no evidence for anyone to conclude otherwise. They embrace people of African descent from the diaspora with open arms and do everything they can to make them feel welcome.

Our research reveals that Africans in general are always on the lookout for opportunities to connect and interact with their counterparts and will go out of their way to make sure they feel welcome. This is especially true of the younger generation in both the urban and rural communities. Hip hop conscious, Internet savvy, ambitious and aggressive, the younger generation of Africans search for ways to connect with people from black communities in America who look like them, whose music, fashion, lingo, and almost everything they do is considered 'cool' and imitated around the globe. Aware of the impact made by African American hip hop culture globally, they make every effort to keep up with the trends through social media. Facebook and other social media make it possible for them to connect and interact online, but they always welcome the chance to make a personal connection. They figure such a connection with African Americans might become useful in the future in any number of ways, most commonly as a stepping stone to building a relationship that can be used as a resource when they decide to travel to Europe or America. More importantly, they are elated to have the chance to interact with people who look like them, but don't speak their language or know about their customs and traditions, yet easily bond with them when they get the chance to interact with each other. They also search for and make the effort to connect with people from the Caribbean whose lifestyle, music, fashion, lingo, food and entertainment are just as unique, distinctive and different, and more relevant to the African experience in many ways. The Rasta influence in Africa is just as pervasive and widespread and has been described as more powerful than hip-hop culture for a number of reasons, not the least of which is the fact that the underlying themes in the Rasta ideology refer to poverty, oppression, struggle for freedom and equality, issues that resonate with Africans today and are real life situations they deal with on a daily basis.

The indisputable fact is this: African-Americans and others of African descent from the diaspora who return to African countries for whatever reason are shown genuine love, appreciation and respect by the African people. Africans treat them like kings and queens in the cities, towns and villages. If it changes, it is because they are given reasons to do so as a result of the attitude or behavior of an individual or group of people. Otherwise, the majority always remain receptive to embracing and welcoming people of African descent from the diaspora in their midst. Many people of African descent from different parts of the world have travelled to Africa and returned home with stories of their overwhelmingly positive experiences and fond memories of being embraced and made to feel at home by Africans in Africa.

AFRICAN AMERICANS AND OTHER PEOPLE OF AFRICAN DESCENT IN THE DIASPORA PROTEST LAWS IN AFRICAN COUNTRIES THAT MAKE IT DIFFICULT, EVEN IMPOSSIBLE FOR THEM TO BECOME CITIZENS

Problem is that the returning men and women of African descent from the diaspora want more than the mere sense of being made to feel welcome and at home by the general African population. They want official government recognition and formal support that would lead to citizenship and place them on a more solid footing in the African countries they repatriate to. They want to feel total acceptance along with the sense of being safe and secure that comes with it.

It has been pointed out by many on social media that African governments make it difficult, if not impossible for African Americans and others of African lineage to repatriate to African countries. They cite policies and regulations that essentially hinder and even disqualify them in some instances, from becoming citizens of African countries. It is a major issue partly because it's viewed as a huge disincentive to those who want to return to Africa. It doesn't make any sense, as far as they are concerned. If anything, it should be the opposite. Over the years,various organizations and many prominent individuals have taken the initiative and asked African governments to do everything possible to encourage African Americans and make the process much easier for those who want to return to live in Africa and contribute to its development. They want African governments to receive, welcome them and make them feel at home, and ultimately provide a pathway to citizenship for those who want to become citizens of African countries.

According to them, government policies as they currently exist, make it difficult and often impossible for African Americans and others of African lineage to aspire to attain citizenship in African countries. And citizenship in African countries is precisely what they want more than anything else. They don't understand the reason why African governments have policies that appear to make it difficult for people of African descent around the world to return to the land of their ancestry, yet don't apply the same restrictions to Europeans and Americans. Advocates who have aligned themselves with the movement for the return of people of African descent to Africa have raised similar objections. They have called on African countries to enact new laws and regulations that would make it easier for them to repatriate to African countries with the expectation that they would become citizens if they want to. They cite the benefits to be reaped by African countries who open their doors for people of African descent in the diaspora. They have the potential to play an important role in the development of the countries in which they settle.

GHANA GOVERNMENT HAS TAKEN THE INITIATIVE

The Ghana government has responded and announced plans to encourage and ultimately make it a lot less difficult for African Americans to repatriate to the country. It currently offers the "Right of Abode" program which allows people of African descent to gain permanent residency if they decide to repatriate. According to the Ghanaian Immigration Act of 2000, "The concept of right of abode under Immigration Law is that person having the right of abode shall be free to live and to come and go into and from the country without let or hindrance."

It has been in effect for almost two decades, but appears to be relatively unknown. In 2019, the right of abode law in Ghana moved into center stage as one of the key components of the Year of Return. It provides the answer to the question of what is involved in the process of repatriating to Africa for people of Africa in the diaspora. In essence, it addresses some of their major concerns. What happens after repatriating to an African country in terms of permanent residency, land and property ownership? Do African Americans and others of African lineage have the same rights and privileges? Would they have any reason to be concerned about potential problems with living in Africa? Ghana's initiative makes it a lot easier for someone like Ras Lawrence to make the decision of returning to Africa to live on a permanent basis. He knows for sure that Ghana is making the effort to welcome and embrace him and others who are seriously considering repatriating to Africa. Not surprisingly, his focus is on Ghana, with plans to expand his business and social enterprises into other African countries.

"It is appropriate that Ghana has enacted such a law as the Right of Abode. It will definitely help most of us that are thinking of repatriating to Africa to feel more secure and less hesitant in making the decision to go back to Africa," said Ras Lawrence, the Syracuse based Jamaican who has made the decision to repatriate to an African country. Permanent residency leading to full citizenship has been one of his main concerns.

CHAPTER ELEVEN

STEREOTYPES AND MISCONCEPTIONS AFRICANS HAVE ABOUT EUROPEANS, AMERICANS AND PEOPLE FROM OTHER CONTINENTS

It goes both ways when it comes to stereotypes and misconceptions. Africans also have their own stereotypes and misconceptions about Americans, Europeans and people from other continents and races and interact with them on the basis of what they presume to know about them.

The stereotypes and misconceptions are based on their experiences with other people from different races, but mostly as a result of their interactions with them during the era of colonialism in Africa.

We must note here that the scope of this book does not allow us to discuss the subject of the impact of colonialism on the cultures of Africa in any detail for readers to understand the role colonialism played in the creation and perpetuation of the various stereotypes and misconceptions about Europeans and Americans that Africans have about them. That is for the history books. Suffice it to say that colonialism was a period in history when the African continent was colonized and ruled by European countries and impacted Africans and the educational systems that trained and provided them with skills and professions, the financial infrastructure that controlled their resources, and the economic and social institutions that regulated the way they lived.

As a result, colonialism has become part of the legacy of most people in Africa and provided the background for most of the stereotypes and misconceptions that Africans have about people from other races partly because many of them were created during the period in history when many African countries were under the influence of various European countries.

Just as significant is the fact that for centuries, Europeans and Americans have been involved in trade and commerce of all types with African countries. For instance, Liberia in West Africa was a major source of rubber to the United States. To facilitate the process of the production of rubber, Firestone, an American company that dominated the tire industry, set up plantations and factories that were run and managed by Americans who lived there as expatriates, creating entire communities. Interaction between Africans and Americans led to the emergence of certain stereotypes and misconceptions that continue to be told.

Similar situations in different parts of Africa gave rise to various stereotypes and misconceptions about Europeans and Americans in Africa. Here are a few you might already know about.

ALL AMERICANS AND EUROPEANS THAT GO TO AFRICA FOR WHATEVER REASON ARE RICH. WELL TO DO AND HAVE LOTS OF DOLLARS AND EUROS TO SPEND

This is a huge misconception that appears to characterize the way many Africans perceive Europeans and Americans who travel to Africa. The majority of Europeans and Americans who travel to Africa are not rich and well to do; at least, not all of them consider themselves to be rich in the sense of having lots of money in the bank or having assets that are valued in the millions. But as far as the majority of Africans are concerned, most Europeans and Americans who travel to Africa are loaded with cash and tend to deal with them on that basis. What they don't know is that Europeans and Americans and, for that matter, most people from other countries who visit, repatriate or become expatriates in Africa are ordinary people and not necessarily rich or well to do. Indeed, many are ordinary people who make the decision to go to Africa, plan how to do it and go about it the same way other people do when they plan to do something; they save their money. Problem is, most Africans don't know that. They have preconceived notions based on what they know about Europeans and Americans in the past, and their general behavior.

Again, we have to refer to history and the impact of colonialism on Africa and Africans to illustrate the origin of one of the most common misconceptions about Europeans and Americans in Africa. The presence of European powers during the colonial era and American expatriates in Africa had an immense effect on the natives in terms of exposing them to the outside world, and quite often making it possible for many of them to get to know about them and their lifestyle. The educational systems, religions, recreational activities and the arts and cultures to a remarkable degree in most African countries were based on European models that had the effect of familiarizing and influencing the natives to relate to Europe and America in a way that reinforced values alien to them. It was not uncommon to find Africans more inclined to assimilating the ways and mannerisms of their European colonialists rather than embracing their own cultures.

Even today, the American or European expatriate in Africa is a common sight. They can be seen in rural communities as well as the metropolitan urban areas. They're diplomats, business people, teachers and others in various professional positions whose expertise, knowledge and experience qualify them to get high profile jobs and lucrative contracts to work for their governments, foreign governments, companies and nongovernmental organizations on salaries that allow them to continue to live a comfortable and affluent lifestyle.

EUROPEANS AND AMERICAN EXPATRIATES IN AFRICA LIVE IN GRAND STYLE IN MANSIONS AND PALATIAL HOMES WITH AFRICANS AS DOMESTIC SERVANTS

It is not unusual for an expatriate European or American in Africa to employ a crew of Africans to provide certain services, especially in their homes. They live in palatial homes built or rented by the companies that employ them that are relatively cheap to maintain, using local labor. The local labor force is abundant and extremely cheap by American and European standards, making it easy for the average expatriate to live in grand style, all their needs taken care of by African servants, maids, cooks, drivers, chauffeurs, and houseboys, etc.

CHEAP DOMESTIC LABOR IS ABUNDANT IN AFRICA AND MAKES IT POSSIBLE FOR EUROPEAN AND AMERICAN EXPATRIATES TO LIVE LUXURIOUS LIFESTYLES THEY CAN'T AFFORD BACK HOME.

The majority of European and American expatriates in Africa depend on cheap domestic labor to take care of the upkeep and maintenance of their homes. It is a common practice for an American and European expatriate to hire an entire staff of Africans at a residence charged with the responsibility of taking care of the various needs of the expatriate boss. For many expatriates, the domestic staff may consist of a driver, security guard, garden boy whose main duty is to take care of the gardens, flowers, and the grounds, and a cook who is in charge of the kitchen and all culinary arrangements. It's possible for European and American expatriates to hire and pay for the different services provided by various people because all the salaries of the entire native domestic staff can be covered by a small percentage of the salary of their expatriate employer. That has been the general lifestyle of Europeans and Americans in Africa for centuries. It continues today in slightly different ways, but essentially the same in terms of the availability of cheap local help.

AMERICANS AND EUROPEANS WHO TRAVEL TO AFRICA FOR VACATION AND SAFARIS AND GAME HUNTING STAY IN LUXURY HOTELS. DINE IN TOP RESTAURANTS AND BUY EXPENSIVE GIFTS FOR FAMILY AND FRIENDS. MAKING IT LOOK LIKE THEY HAVE LOTS OF MONEY TO SPEND.

When Europeans and Americans go to Africa for whatever reason, they check into the best and most expensive hotels, dine at the top restaurants and do things that make it seem as though they have lots of money. Thus the image of the affluent white foreigner is reinforced in Africa in modern times by ordinary men and women who travel there on budgets with no intention of pretending to be rich or well to do. They may have just about enough to buy a tour package and obtain sufficient foreign exchange to be able to enjoy their vacation, and basically do what most people do back home with their discretionary income. They may be just hard working middle class people who made plans to go overseas for their vacation, chose Africa for reasons best known to them and brought enough funds to cover hotel and other related expenses. As far as they are concerned, they are not doing anything extraordinary that should elevate them to the status of the rich and well to do. They have no idea that the ordinary vacation related things they do in Africa have the effect of projecting them as having more than enough to spend. On the other hand, the majority of Africans have no way of knowing that most of the Americans and Europeans who visit Africa as tourists are ordinary hardworking people who have no intention of pretending to be rich. They just happen to have enough foreign exchange to cover their travel expenses and really don't care what Africans think.

THERE ARE NO POOR WHITE PEOPLE IN MOST AFRICAN COUNTRIES. ONLY A FEW COUNTRIES WITH LARGE WHITE POPULATIONS HAVE WHITE PEOPLE WHO MAY BE DESCRIBED AS POOR

A white person whose appearance and demeanor bespeak of abject poverty is practically nonexistent in Africa. Most Africans, especially from West Africa, have not seen a really destitute, poverty stricken, homeless white person begging on a street corner or wandering aimlessly about. Indeed, no such sighting of a poor white person is likely to occur simply because it doesn't exist in most African countries. It's no surprise that the majority of Africans in Africa seem to think that there are no poor white people. What they don't know is that homelessness and extreme poverty are common in European and American cities. The only exception may be in a few countries in Africa, especially South Africa, that have a large concentration of European settlers who have lived there for generations and consider themselves as Africans. Even among them, the incidence of extreme poverty is not common. More often than not, they are the beneficiaries of what has come to be known as white privilege and are not likely to be extremely poor and deprived.

"We don't see any poor white Americans and Europeans in Africa. It doesn't mean there are no poor white people. Poor, jobless and financially deprived white people just don't come to Africa," said George Mensah of Nyanyano in the Central Region of Ghana. He knows what he's talking about. He immigrated to the United States from Ghana in the late seventies and lived in Newark, New Jersey for three decades. Homeless white people with no places they could call their own were common. So were desperately poor white people who had no jobs, no income and survived in the streets. He returned to Ghana and lives in a community that has evolved from a small fishing community into a thriving township with all the attendant urban settings as a result of its close proximity to Accra, the capital city of Ghana. It used to be a favorite location for European and American expatriates for weekend getaways. They rolled into town on Saturdays and Sundays in their cars, brought gifts of books and toys to the kids and went to the beach and enjoyed themselves. He doesn't recall seeing any poor white person in Ghana before he immigrated overseas. The point he makes is essentially true. Europeans and Americans who live in Africa are mostly professionals with high paying jobs. They wouldn't have travelled to Africa if they didn't have such a high paying job to begin with and the money and resources that come with it.

ALL EUROPEANS AND AMERICANS ARE EDUCATED, GENEROUS AND COMPASSIONATE

In most African countries, the notion of the benevolent Europeans and Americans is a common misconception. Europeans, Americans and other Caucasians are held in high esteem and regarded as kind, compassionate and giving. It's no mystery how that misconception developed. As alluded to elsewhere, the European or American expatriates in Africa tend to be people in high positions in government, business and nongovernmental organizations and have access to enough resources to be able to live the affluent lifestyle in Africa. Back home in their native countries, most wouldn't be able to afford the kind of lifestyle they live in Africa, if they had no other sources of funds besides their salaries from their employment. But they are able to live the grand lifestyle in Africa for the simple reason that labor costs are low, especially domestic labor. They hire and pay local labor as drivers, gardeners, cooks and are able to pay them reasonably decent wages by local standards.

Interestingly enough, only Africans in Africa appear to subscribe to the notion of the benevolent American or European. African-Americans, people of African heritage from the Caribbean and elsewhere around the world totally disagree with Africans and have not shied away from pointing out how naïve and clueless Africans are to believe that all Europeans and Americans are generous, benevolent and giving. They perceive Americans and Europeans as the most cruel and inhumane people on earth and blame them for dispossessing Africa and Africans of their wealth and natural resources through conquest and colonization of the continent. They point out that Europeans and Americans have succeeded in projecting that kind of image in Africa and engage in acts of kindness in part became they control and manage various humanitarian activities. Those familiar with business management and administrative strategies go as far as to point out that what Africans may consider as acts of kindness may actually be business expenses that may be refunded to them by the organizations and businesses they work for. They simply have more resources to work with and can afford to 'live large' and project an image of affluence, charitableness and benevolence.

FOOD AID AND OTHER FOREIGN AID PROGRAMS REINFORCE THE IMAGE OF THE BENEVOLENT AMERICANS AND EUROPEANS IN AFRICA PARTLY BECAUSE THE MAJORITY OF AFRICANS DON'T KNOW THAT THE PROGRAMS ARE HUMANITARIAN PROJECTS RUN BY NON PROFIT ORGANIZATIONS CONTROLLED BY EUROPEANS AND AMERICANS.

It has also been argued that another source of misconceptions about the generosity of Europeans and Americans is food aid sent to areas in Africa that were affected by starvation and hunger as a result of famine and other forms of natural disasters Most Africans, particularly those in rural areas, have no knowledge about the nature and organizational structures of the various food aid programs and other philanthropic initiatives that deliver food aid and medical supplies when disaster strikes and the need arises for emergency food supplies to be flown in from other countries and continents. They don't know that the food aid comes from organizations that are part of a global network of nongovernmental and nonprofit organizations set up for the purpose of providing assistance to people in need all over the world, funded and administered by Europeans and Americans.

Thus when the call goes out for food aid and the organizations respond, such aid programs are almost always managed by Europeans and Americans. To most rural community based Africans, food aid might seem to be acts of kindness by the Europeans and Americans that are sent to the disaster stricken areas to manage the food distribution. The majority of Africans, especially those in rural areas have no idea that the Europeans and Americans who manage the food aid and other humanitarian programs represent or are a part of a sophisticated network of humanitarian organizations that raises funds to use to finance such food aid programs. Food aid and other humanitarian projects run by Europeans and Americans in Africa, have as one of the unintended consequences the creation of the misconception that Europeans and Americans are always generous and benevolent.

CHAPTER TWELVE

IS AFRICA SAFE?

Is Africa safe is a perfectly legitimate question to ask by anyone planning to travel to the African continent regardless of the reason or for how long. It makes sense to ask questions about safety and security, considering the bad press the African continent has received from the global media over the years.

The glossy brochures and slick advertising campaigns about pyramids, safaris and wild game hunting in Africa do a good job of presenting the African continent in a certain light to people whose interest is premised on the notion that Africa is an exotic continent with unique characteristics that will gratify their quest for extraordinary travel experiences that cannot be found anywhere else. They focus on people whose main reason for traveling to Africa are the pyramids, safari and game hunting and other thrills that are associated with it. They are willing and able to pay the big bucks for that privilege. The glossy magazines and slick television advertisements are specially made for them and provide them with precisely the kind of information they need to make the decision to invest in the tour packages.

Such tour packages to Africa for safari and wild game hunting and pyramid tours are not cheap and tend to be the preserve of the rich and well to do as a result. The safety and security concerns of those who go on such safaris and wild game hunting trips may have more to do with danger posed by being in close proximity to wild animals than anything else.

What about others whose interests have nothing to do with safaris, game hunting and pyramid tours? What about those who seek to experience the culture, history, and the people of the African continent? How safe and secure will they be if they venture out on their own to try to get a sense of what other aspects of Africa and Africans are about?

Contrary to what is generally said and written about Africa as a dangerous and primitive continent, Africa is one of the safest continents to travel to for any purpose. Many people from different races around the globe have done so and have written about the wonderful time they had. The friendliness, geniality and readiness of the Africans made them feel welcome and at home. More importantly, they felt safe and secure and didn't have to take any extraordinary measures to protect themselves.

TRAVELING TO AFRICA IS BASICALLY THE SAME WHEN IT COMES TO THE BASICS ABOUT SAFETY AND SECURITY CONCERNS IN ANY FOREIGN COUNTRY

Traveling to Africa basically involves just about everything one would have to deal with when it comes to visiting any other continent. All the fundamental rules and regulations that apply elsewhere to safety and security concerns apply in similar situations in Africa. It makes sense to use caution when you travel to a foreign city and are visiting places you don't know. It is one of the most common safety and security hints to be found in most travel and tourism related publications.

AFRICA IS A RELATIVELY SAFE AND SECURE CONTINENT

For those in the process of traveling to Africa and aren't sure about their safety and security in their chosen destination, it's a good idea to check travel warnings. They are issued by governments and provide relevant information and data about the safety and security conditions in other countries. African countries are always included in such listings and can be easily obtained. Again, staying safe in any foreign country is usually a matter of common sense. There are, of course, some regions or countries that are legitimately unsafe for tourists. Quite often, such areas tend to be known to the public as a result of the media coverage about the wars, conflicts or other factors that have created those unsafe conditions.

The general observation has been that Africa is essentially safe to travel to for the purposes of visiting and touring, or taking up residence as an expatriate or 'returning' for African Americans who have made the decision to repatriate.

The large majority of travelers to Africa return home or live there without encountering any serious problems. This is not to say that one should assume that it is a perfectly safe environment. No continent can claim to be totally safe and secure for people who travel there. Like other continents, there are certain areas that are known to be strife torn and unsafe to travel to for any reason. It makes sense not to go to those areas, at least not when they are in the midst of conflicts that have not been resolved.

SUGGESTIONS ON SAFETY AND SECURITY: CERTAIN AFRICAN COUNTRIES CONSIDERED TO BE LESS THAN SAFE AND SECURE

Some countries like the Central African Republic, Sudan, Somalia or Libya are among the world's most dangerous because of conflicts, crime and terrorist related activities, and should be avoided at all costs, mostly for safety and security reasons, at least for now. The Central Sahara region is now partly controlled by Al Qaeda. In northern Mali, near the Nigerian border and Mauritania, several kidnappings have occurred, as well as a number of suicide bombings.

SPECIFIC ACTIONS TO TAKE TO MINIMIZE RISK, PROTECT PROPERTY AND AVOID SECURITY AND SAFETY MISHAPS IN AFRICA

Travel writers and observers of trends in the travel industry have studied security and safety issues in Africa over the years and have put together a list of suggestions designed to guide visitors on the basic steps to take that would make them feel safer, protect them from harm and alert them to situations that have the potential to put them at risk when they travel to the African continent.

The following suggestions are the most common and are designed basically to serve as guidelines for those who place safety and security as a top priority and want to make sure they have done everything within their power to prevent any potential risks.

- Travelers are advised to carry as little cash as possible. The less cash visitors have on them at any particular time, the better. Visitors are also advised to be careful about the amount of cash they carry on their person when they go out in the streets. In Africa, it is possible to shop, pay bills in restaurants, hotels, and do all kinds of transactions in a manner that does not call for immediate access to a lot of cash. Modern technology takes care of that. Even in the remotest regions of Africa, it is now possible to do everything you want to do that involves the use of funds.

- Keep cash out of sight and easy reach. Keeping a wallet in the back pocket is considered a risky way to carry cash when traveling. Visitors are advised to avoid exposing their cash that way.

- Beware of individuals who act strangely and who try to divert your attention in order to steal your belongings.

- Pay special attention while sitting in restaurants and café terraces, when withdrawing money from ATMs or near tourist attractions. Any unusual interest from anyone in what a visitor is doing should be seen as a warning signal.

- Never keep mobile phone or wallet on the table of a café or restaurant.

- Don't wear expensive jewelry in an ostentatious way.

- If an attacker tries to snatch your bag, don't try to stop them. You will risk being injured by anyone desperate and determined to carry out the act of snatching your bag.

- Protect personal belongings at all times, especially ID and passport. Petty crime, like bag snatching and pickpocketing, is a serious problem around tourist areas and on public transport.

TRAVEL BROCHURES AND MAGAZINES DON'T PROVIDE ENOUGH INFORMATION AND DATA ABOUT AFRICA. THEY MOSTLY SELL TOUR PACKAGES ON SAFARI AND WILD GAME HUNTING IN AFRICA

It is not enough to rely on the travel brochures for realistic information about Africa. Those interested in knowing the real deal about Africa need to look further. More than likely, most travel brochures about Africa will focus mainly on promoting pyramid tours, safaris and game hunting in East Africa, make little or no reference to the rest of Africa and present everything else in the context of Africa as the continent that specializes in safari and wildlife. They make it seem as though all you need are big bucks and everything else would be taken care of, including safety and security arrangements. The problem is that a considerable number of people travel to Africa for other reasons that have nothing to do with safari and wild game hunting or the ancient monuments and need the kind of information that will provide insight and guidelines on what they have to do to maximize their African experience and how to feel safe and secure.

CHAPTER THIRTEEN

WHY GO TO AFRICA?

Many people visit particular countries and continents for special reasons. The motivation to visit a country or city on foreign soil for the majority of people derives mostly from the historical significance the place holds for them in terms of their ethnic, racial and cultural heritage. They may not have any direct or immediate connection to the place they want to visit. Nevertheless, they find a compelling reason to go there in part because it has a special meaning for them.

It is for the same reason that African Americans and others of African descent from many different countries around the globe travel to Africa. Africa is special to them. It is the continent of their heritage, ancestry and lineage.

For many Americans, certain countries in Europe have that kind of appeal and inform the decisions made by families and individuals when it comes to travelling overseas. Italy is such a country. It is a popular destination for many Americans who trace their origins to that country. They go there for the simple reason that it is their ancestral home. They trace their roots to Italy and want to go there to reconnect with their people. Similarly, France, Germany, Holland, Poland, the United Kingdom, among others, attract a large number of visitors from around the world whose main reason for going there is the fact that their families immigrated to other parts of the world from those countries.

AFRICA WELCOMES AFRICAN AMERICANS AND ALL OTHERS FROM THE AFRICAN DIASPORA

Africa has that attraction for many African Americans, West Indians and others who trace their origins to Africa.

For African-Americans like Empressima Ethiopia, Tashame Ali, Peter Wynn, Ras Lawrence and many others, Africa is the motherland. They were born and raised in different parts of America, have had widely differing lifestyles and life experiences, but they all relate to Africa in that context like the majority of African-Americans and others of African lineage all over the world when it comes to the continent they consider as their real roots. They are proud to proclaim their connection to Africa as the motherland. For many African Americans that relationship ultimately leads to a decision to reconnect with Africa in a personal way by visiting or repatriating to an African country.

Empressima Ethiopia has made many trips to Africa and has lived in several African countries. She has travelled extensively all over the continent, exploring business opportunities, setting up businesses and creating awareness about the need for African Americans to reconnect with Africa and Africans. Tashame Ali's ultimate goal is to travel to Africa and is actively pursuing plans to make it happen. Peter Wynn and Ras Lawrence have committed themselves to making the journey to Africa and are in the process of doing so. Both have made substantial advancements with their plans. Ras Lawrence has already made the decision to repatriate to Africa and is making arrangements to be able to make the transition to life in Africa.

AFRICA IS THE MOTHERLAND TO AFRICAN AMERICANS AND OTHERS OF AFRICAN LINEAGE FROM AROUND THE WORLD

To the majority of Europeans and Americans, Africa is the land of the pyramids and other ancient monuments, safari and wild game hunting. To African Americans and others of African lineage from the Caribbean and other parts of the world, it is the homeland, the continent to return to when they decide to reconnect with their heritage by way of a visit. Many make the decision to repatriate to an African country when they make up their minds to end the misery, pain, bias and racial prejudice they associate with living in America, Europe or elsewhere.

AFRICA HAS A LONG HISTORY OF WELCOMING FOREIGNERS IN SPITE OF THEIR EXPERIENCE WITH SLAVERY AND EXPLOITATION BY PEOPLE FROM OTHER RACES

Africa has an extraordinarily long history of welcoming and providing a home for expatriates, foreigners, and people of African descent from Europe and America who repatriate to the continent they refer to as the motherland.

African governments and leaders have encouraged foreigners to visit, explore business opportunities and invest and strive to provide an environment that is safe and secure. Governments as well as the general population do everything in their power to make foreigners welcome. The willingness to embrace foreigners on the part of Africans has been blamed for creating various problems that have contributed to the underdevelopment and exploitation of the continent by people of other races. Slavery of Africans by European powers and Arabs continues to be cited as one of the major problems

Africans have had to deal with as a result of welcoming strangers in their midst.

GHANA LAUNCHES THE 'YEAR OF RETURN' INITIATIVE IN 2019 TO ENCOURAGE AFRICAN AMERICANS AND PEOPLE OF AFRICAN DESCENT IN OTHER PARTS OF THE WORLD TO RETURN TO VISIT OR LIVE IN AFRICA

The Ghana government has taken the initiative and launched the Year of Return initiative, a year-long series of activities in 2019 designed to include visits to heritage sites, healing ceremonies, theatre and musical performances, lectures, investment forums and relocation conferences.

It is a major component of a strategy that aims at making Ghana a major tourist destination with a focus on encouraging African Americans and people of African descent to visit or repatriate to the African continent.

2019 marks the 400-year anniversary of the first enslaved Africans' arrival in Jamestown in America. The Year of Return represents an effort to reunite Africans on the continent with their brothers and sisters in the diaspora in a historical context that highlighs the role played by slavery.

Over the years, Ghana has played a leading role in efforts to encourage African Americans to connect with their African heritage. It's independence in 1957 was touted as a victory not just for the country: the African continent and people of African descent all over the world were encouraged, inspired and given reason to believe that they can accomplish the same objective. The global media hype put the spotlight on Ghana, making it the country to visit for African diasporans who wanted to experience life in a post-independence African country.

Many well-known African diasporans visited Ghana in response to an invitation by President Kwame Nkrumah. They included Julian Bond, Martin Luther King Jr., George Padmore, Malcolm X, Maya Angelou, Richard Wright, Leslie Lacy, Muhammad Ali and W.E.B. Du Bois. Others less well known were among those who visited the newly independent nation.

In the 1990s, Ghana's President Jerry Rawlings initiated a heritage tourism strategy based on the transatlantic slave trade and Pan-Africanism. The coastal forts and castles were presented as key elements to promote the heritage based tourism. Events included the Pan African Festival of Theatre and Arts (PANAFEST) and Emancipation Day. All were dedicated to the promotion of Pan-Africanism and attracted African diasporans, notably African Americans.

As part of the nation's 50th independence in 2007, President John Kuffour partnered with the Discovery Channel and launched "Ghana – The Presidential Tour". He introduced "The Joseph Project" that targeted middle-class Christian African Americans.

The forts and castles remained a significant aspect of the initiative. Additional plans included the development of commemoration gardens, DNA projects and sponsored tours. It also involved developing an interfaith center to memorialize how captive Africans had their last bath before being transported onto the slave ships.

President John Atta Mills continued with heritage tourism. In 2009, the most high-profile African diasporan, US President Barack Obama, visited Ghana.

In 2015, President John Mahama sought assistance from the United Nations Educational, Scientific and Cultural Organization as part of the overall strategy for further development of heritage tourism.

Over the years, successive governments have also offered opportunities such as granting citizenship, dual nationality status, tax exemptions and land grants to diasporans to encourage returnees.

The goal of the Year of Return remains the same: to continue to promote heritage based tourism and make 2019 the year that many people of African descent in the diaspora visit or repatriate to Africa as a result of the active support, involvement and encouragement from African governments.

CHAPTER FOURTEEN

DEALING WITH CULTURAL, SOCIAL, ECONOMIC AND POLITICAL DIFFERENCES BETWEEN AFRICANS AND AFRICAN AMERICANS AND OTHERS OF AFRICAN DESCENT WHO TRAVEL OR REPATRIATE TO AFRICA

How smooth is the transition from life in urban America for African Americans who decide to repatriate to Africa? Do people of African descent from other parts of the globe face similar, more or less problems when they visit or repatriate to Africa? What kind of problems do they face when it comes to interacting and relating to the African people?

Such questions are not easy to answer in part because the potential problems to be faced or actual problems encountered by those who have experienced them have not been widely discussed. The subject is considered to be irrelevant and not worth talking about. As far as the majority of Africans and African Americans are concerned, they get along just fine. They don't need anyone or anything to remind them otherwise about any potential problems or difficulties to be overcome. The focus is more on what has to be done to strengthen ties, build bridges and reunite all people of African descent the world over. Regardless, the reality for most is that sometimes they are forced to deal with the feeling of being different in a number of ways when they have to interact and reach out to the people as part of the process of integrating into the African communities in which they find themselves.

AFRICAN AMERICANS AND OTHER DIASPORAN AFRICANS SUCCESSFULLY INTEGRATE INTO AFRICAN COMMUNITIES IN SPITE OF LANGUAGE AND CULTURAL DIFFERENCES

Quite often, they are reminded in subtle and sometimes not so subtle ways that they can't speak any African language, don't understand and can't relate to the various African cultures as a result of being born and raised in different cultures and have acquired different values and characteristics that define them and shape the way they see and do things.

In the eyes of some of the Africans, their inability to communicate in the local language puts them on the same footing with Europeans and Americans and gives them a reason to refer to them by such names as 'oburoni' in Ghana which basically means a white person.

These are some of the questions that come to mind in certain situations for African Americans and other diasporan Africans who travel to Africa. How do they deal with the fact that the majority of Africans view and react to African Americans the same way they do with white Americans and Europeans? How do they feel about not knowing what tribe or nationality they belong to in Africa?

Again, it's not been easy searching for answers, partly because the subject of how Africans and African-Americans feel and interact with each other is a non-issue as far as the majority is concerned. A far more pressing and immediate issue that overshadows everything else and most feel compelled to discuss is the racial divide between people of color and the white majority and the problems we all have to contend with as a result being black in Africa, America, Europe and elsewhere.

Generally, African-Americans and Africans acknowledge a powerful bonding and a sense of oneness regardless of where any kind of interaction occurs or the circumstances. Perhaps of more significance is the ever present feeling of being forced to feel different as a result of being black in an environment in which white dominance is a major characteristic. It creates a sense of marginalization not easy to overcome, or ignore. Just as powerful and pervasive is the feeling that people of African descent consider themselves as belonging to one universal tribe with their African heritage as the most important and relevant component.

INCREASING NUMBERS OF AFRICAN AMERICANS AND PEOPLE OF AFRICAN DESCENT AROUND THE GLOBE ARE REPATRIATING TO AFRICA AS A RESULT OF RENEWED INTEREST IN AFRICA

In a wider context, the enthusiasm and excitement generated by the repatriation to Africa movement is seen as an indication that people of African descent all over the world remain conscious of the notion that they have the option to return to Africa if they want to. They recognize the fact that they happen to be spread all over the world, not by choice in most instances, but by circumstances beyond their control. Their origins go back to Africa, no matter where they happen to be. Their main concern is what happens when they get there. They consider themselves as having the right to return to Africa, and expect to be welcomed and embraced wherever they decide to go on the African continent.

HOW AFROCENTRIC DIASPORANS VIEW AFRICA AND AFRICANS

That is the view of those who describe themselves as Afrocentric or Pan Africanists. They are African Americans and others of African lineage around the globe who project themselves as unapologetically pro Africa and reinforce that image with the costumes they wear, hairstyles and general lifestyle. They love everything about Africa and Africans, try to learn about African history and culture and include a journey to Africa as one of their priorities in life, likening it to a pilgrimage. The majority of people who have visited or repatriated to Africa tend to belong to that category.

To them, anyone of African descent who holds a different opinion that suggests otherwise risks being seen as a traitor of the race. These are the hardcore, Africa loving people of African descent who assume new names they create themselves, and begin to live lifestyles based on traditional, religious and cultural practices that are completely different from those into which they were born. They are easily identified, often from the manner in which they flaunt their pride in Africa rather aggressively, in the privacy of their homes and in public.

Meanwhile, studies have been cited that have revealed that Africans in America, African-Americans, West Indians and other black people in the diaspora are dissimilar culturally, socially, economically and politically. And that poses a challenge to those who have repatriated or are thinking about doing so. According to the sceptics, skin color is just about the most common characteristic between them. Beyond that, they have very little in common.

In many instances, they may have to deal with situations that might make them feel as though they are different, misunderstood and even unwelcome in Africa. Consequently, African Americans and others from the Diaspora who had high hopes of transitioning to a continent they regard as their homeland have to deal with mixed feelings that may not be easy to overcome.

HOW EUROCENTRIC DIASPORAN AFRICANS VIEW AFRICA AND AFRICANS

It is also true that some African Americans and other diasporan Africans could care less about Africa and Africans and everything else that is supposed to connect them with the African continent. They see themselves as essentially American or Eurocentric, in terms of their values and lifestyles. They feel no compelling need to identify with any other culture other than what they know or were born into, the American or European way of life. They don't relate to Africa in any way, and focus mostly on figuring out how to survive in a country they call their own. They find a more compelling reason to make an effort to be part of the American or European mainstream rather than concern themselves with the notion of making their American or other nationality an issue.

The question becomes; why do people assume that Africans and African-Americans are the same in the first place? The obvious answer is: skin color and everything else associated with it.

Interestingly enough, the problems that racism and bigotry have created for people of Africa and African descent over the years all over the world appear to be issues that people want to discuss. They are more interested in finding out what can be done to unite black people globally and make Africa strong, safe, and secure so people of African descent can visit or repatriate to the African continent.

CHAPTER FIFTEEN

WHAT TO DO ABOUT FOOD

As improbable as it may seem, food can become an issue for people from the African diaspora who find themselves in any part of Africa as expatriates, visitors or returnees who have repatriated with plans to make Africa their new home. Regardless of the duration or the reason for going to Africa, the question almost always arises: what to do about food? For returnees who live or plan to live in African communities for an extended period, it can become an issue for which they have to find a solution. They have to make decisions on the most mundane issue that everyone ever has to deal with: food

Usually three options present themselves in such a situation.

1. Get into the habit of eating local dishes and foods, and cooking dishes and cuisine that are common and popular in the country and culture in that particular African country. There are variations in the dietary and culinary traditions in different parts of Africa. Certain dishes that are common in West Africa may not be as popular in East Africa and vice versa. For instance, two popular dishes, Jollof rice and couscous are popular in West Africa, but are not part of the staple diet in other parts of Africa. It takes time and effort to get used to the different dishes and cuisines.

2.   Stick with what they know and make no attempt to accommodate eating habits and foods in the new environment in Africa. And that is not too difficult to do these days. It is not a totally helpless situation for those who just don't care for or simply can't seem to develop an appetite for local and traditional African dishes and prefer to continue with what they know. We'll explain how that has been made possible with the emergence of ethnic and specialty grocery stores all over Africa.

3.   Combine dishes and food items from the culture in which they were born and raised with African dishes and food items. It simply means experimenting with new and different dishes, cuisine and food items and making the best of it. Preferred by many, this is the approach usually used by immigrants from different countries who settle in Europe and America and has resulted in the creation of a wide range of unique dishes, cooking and eating patterns in many parts of the world.

NOT AN EASY TRANSITION FOR PEOPLE OF AFRICAN DESCENT BORN AND RAISED IN AMERICA AND EUROPE WHEN IT COMES TO FOOD

Changing their eating habits as a result of traveling to or living in an African country presents a challenge to most people not born and raised there. With tastes firmly established from back home in America or Europe, they may find it difficult to abandon their style of cooking, eating habits and cuisine in favor of African style cooking and cuisine. Even if they make the effort, in response to the need to try to conform, making the transition as part of the process of mainstreaming into the native culture takes time, but may ultimately produce some results. It is not easy by any stretch of the imagination.

NO CAN DO IS THE ATTITUDE OF MANY AFRICAN AMERICANS WHO RELOCATE

Others may either just refuse to try anything they don't know about or don't feel comfortable with and blame it on a number of factors. The most common reason is that African dishes are too spicy.

To such people, visiting, repatriating or immigrating to Africa does not mean changing one's eating habits, at least not immediately. They don't see a change in eating habits as a necessary part of the process of feeling at home in an African environment. It has no cultural significance the way it does for others. They don't have a compelling need or desire to substitute the old with something new.

This is the type of individual who makes a conscious and concerted effort to keep old habits alive by continuing to practice them. They are not willing to make any compromises, if they don't have to.

It is to be expected that anyone born and raised in America or Europe who travels to Africa will be slow in adapting to local dietary and eating habits. Pride in Africa heritage notwithstanding, an African American who is new to Africa and not too familiar with the local traditional cuisine is not likely to make an effort to learn to cook Nigerian or Ghanaian dishes immediately in part because they are totally different from what they know.

INTERNATIONAL AND SPECIALTY GROCERY STORES MAKE IT POSSIBLE TO CONTINUE WITH OLD EATING HABITS IN AFRICA

Luckily, African Americans and others from the African diaspora are able to maintain their old eating habits in Africa mainly as a result of another aspect of the globalization of the international community, brought about partly by immigration around the world. In most African cities, businesses that describe themselves as international or specialty grocery stores make it possible to obtain food ingredients from different parts of the world, especially Europe and America. They import food items that are distributed, marketed and promoted with European and Americsn communities in mind.

These cater specifically to a market created as a result of the presence of European and American expatriates and immigrants in most African countries. Located mostly in large cities, they are usually operated by immigrant families and stock all kinds of food items and specialty products.

They advertise and promote themselves in various ways; as import and export businesses in the large metropolitan areas and sell other ethnic based consumer products besides food items such as furniture, clothing, etc. Recent media reports indicate that in most cities in Africa, the trend has shifted towards building large grocery stores that cater to expatriate Europeans and Americans and people from other races. They create and maintain sections dedicated to foreign foods, giving people from other countries the choice to shop for food items that can be used to prepare a variety of dishes foreign to Africa.

Pizza comes to mind as a typical foreign food item that has become quite popular in Africa. Restaurants in African cities include it as one of their specialties and the ingredients that are used to prepare it are sold in many outlets in most African cities.

MIXING IT UP AND CREATING NEW DISHES AS A RESULT: CREATIVE COOKING IN AFRICA

The third option is basically an exercise in creative cooking. Here an attempt is made to blend the two worlds that have come together as a result of living in an African community and trying to be part of it. The need to create something not too different from what they know is the motivating factor for those who make an effort to combine the two cultures. Most succeed in doing so, though it requires a considerable degree of culinary dexterity.

RICE IS THE MOST COMMON STAPLE FOOD IN AFRICA AND EASY TO ADAPT BY THOSE WHO TRY CREATIVE COOKING IN AFRICA

Rice comes to mind as one food item that can be easily adapted. One of the most popular staple foods consumed by most people from different parts of the world, it is widely accepted that the way in which it is prepared is what makes it different. Flavored and cooked in a slightly different way, the end product usually comes out just about right and enough to satisfy all palates.

So are different varieties of stews, soups and breads as well as many other dishes. Here again, the modern international and specialty grocery store plays a role in supplying most of the food items, with the rest available from other sources such as markets. It's all in the cooking: the way it is done, how long it is cooked, and the spices used that contribute to making food taste, feel and look different, making it less of a problem or none at all, in instances where food becomes an issue for anyone who repatriates, visits or immigrates to any African country.

Those visiting might have no problems, especially if they are staying at a hotel. Hotels in African countries usually have restaurants that provide international cuisine that might not be too different from what is available in other parts of the world. African countries now boast some of the world renowned hotel franchises owned and operated by the same hotel chains in other countries. Hotels advertising themselves as 5 star can be seen in most major African cities.

TRADITIONAL AFRICAN DISHES

The foods of Africa are colorful, flavorful, and easily replicated from simple ingredients. Traditionally, the various cuisines of Africa use a combination of locally available fruits such as cereal grains and vegetables. In some parts of the continent, the traditional diet features an abundance of milk, curd and whey products.

In North African cuisine, the most common staple foods are meat, seafood, goat, lamb, beef, dates, almonds, olives, various vegetables and fruit. Because the region is predominantly Muslim, halal meats are usually eaten. The best-known North African/ Berber dish abroad is couscous and tajine.

Couscous is a staple found mainly in North African cuisine. It is steamed semolina usually served with a stew or meat dish. It is a national dish in Algeria, and is a popular accompaniment in Berber traditional dishes. You can find ready-to-eat couscous in most Western supermarkets

Meats in Central Africa cuisine include goat and chicken.

Jollof rice is a great favorite all over West Africa, and often considered to be the origin of the Cajun dish jambalaya.

A simple, spicy one-pot dish comprising, at its most basic, rice, tomatoes, onions and pepper, it's often served at parties and other festive gatherings, along with other favorites such as egusi soup (made with ground melon seeds and bitter leaf), fried plantains and pounded yam (iyan or fufu).

Other dishes include thick, spicy broths made with okra and flavored with chicken or meat, and suya, which are spicy shish kebabs cooked over braziers by street vendors.

Injera is a widely-consumed flatbread found in Ethiopian and Eritrean cuisine. It is the main accompaniment to stews such as zigni and tsebhi stew. Injera is made with teff, a grain widely grown in East Africa and is the healthier substitute for rice, maize and corn. It's made by mixing teff flour and water, and letting the mixture sit for up to 3 days to allow it to ferment.

Fufu is a traditional dish in Western Africa, with many people considering it the most important. Maize, being an ingredient in fufu, is a common ingredient in Western Africa. Couscous is also popular here.

Eastern African cuisine is very interesting, since it is predominantly comprised of starches with much fewer meat options. Maize, or corn, is the main ingredient in the hugely popular and common dish ugali, a starch dish that is eaten with stews and meat. In Uganda, a green banana called a matoke is the source of starch for most meals. Doro Wal, Ethiopian chicken, is a meat-based dish that is eaten with rice and vegetables.

Over time, immigrants have colored the foods of Eastern Africa. The immigrants were predominantly Arab, British, Indian, and Portuguese. The Arabs contributed steamed rice and spices like saffron, cloves, and cinnamon. The British and Indians brought vegetable curries and lentil soups, while the Portuguese were more exotic with their additions of chiles, pineapples, and domestic pigs. Spicy Berbere Lentil Stew is an Eastern African dish that has just the right amount of meat and is a great introduction to this cuisine.

Sometimes called "rainbow cuisine," Southern African foods are a made up of a mix of influences from indigenous tribes, European cuisines and Asian cuisines. There were multiple indigenous tribes in Southern Africa, each with their own culture, language, and cooking style. The largest indigenous group was and remains the Bantu group. They grow crops and raise cattle, sheep, and goats. Today, South Africans enjoy "braai," or South African barbeque. This meal is usually made up of a lot of grilled meat.

EATING WITH FINGERS AND RIGHT HAND IS CUSTOMARY IN MOST AFRICAN COUNTRIES

Food consumption patterns differ in Africa and reflect a variety of influences. In a typical traditional setting in most African communities, food is dished and eaten in ways that conform with tribal customs and mores. For the majority of Africans, sharing a meal means eating from the same bowl with others with one's fingers. That's a major characteristic in most African countries. They make good use of their fingers to eat their food. None of the niceties and table manners of fine dining that are common in Western cultures. Many traditional African foods such as fufu, injera and gari usually can only be eaten with the fingers.

A full course meal in a traditional setting is nothing like what most people born and raised in America or Europe know. When it is time to eat, pieces of fufu, injera or gari are worked into solid balls with the right fingers, dipped into soups and stews made with vegetables, and eaten with the right hand

CHAPTER SIXTEEN

AFRICAN COUNTRIES AT A GLANCE

Africa is a huge and diverse continent that is unique in many different ways. It consists of several countries, ethnic and tribal groups and cultures, making it one of the most fascinating continents in the world. This chapter is not intended to represent a comprehensive profile of African countries. It's more like a listing of the various countries that make up the continent of Africa, with additional information and data on certain aspects of each country's profile that may add context and meaning to what you may already know about the various African countries.

ALGERIA

The largest country in Africa, Algeria is bordered on the east by Tunisia and Libya, on the southeast and south by Niger, on the south and south west by Mali, on the west by Mauritania and on the west, northwest by Morocco. Situated in the northwestern part of the African continent, it is on the northern coastline of the Mediterranean Sea.

For more information, please check this website: https://www.Africaguide.com/country/algeria/

ANGOLA

Angola is bordered on the north by Congo, north and northeast by Dem. Rep. of Congo, formerly Zaire, on the southeast by Zambia and on the south by Namibia and on the west by the Atlantic Ocean.

For more information, please check this website: https://www. Africaguide.com/country/angola/

BENIN

Benin is situated in West Africa on the northern coast of the Gulf of Guinea. It has land borders to the north by Niger, on the west by Togo and on the northwest by Burkina Faso.

For more information, please check this website: https://www. Africaguide.com/country/benin/

BOTSWANA

Botswana is a landlocked country located in Southern Africa. It has land borders with Zimbabwe to the northeast, South Africa to the south and southeast and with Namibia to the west.

For more information, please check this website: https://www. Africaguide.com/country/botswana/

BURKINA FASO

Burkina Faso is a landlocked country in West Africa. It is bordered by Niger in the east, Benin in the southeast, Togo and

Ghana and Ivory Coast in the south, and in the west and north by Mali.

For more information, please check this website:https://www. Africaguide.com/country/ bfasso/

BURUNDI

Burundi is a landlocked country located in east-central Africa. It borders with Rwanda to the north, Tanzania to the east and south and to the west by Zaire.

For more information, please check this website:https://www. Africaguide.com/country/burundi/

CAMEROON

Situated in West Africa, Cameroon is shaped like an elongated triangle. It borders with Chad to the north and northeast, Central African Republic to the east, Congo, Gabon and Equatorial Guinea to the south, the Gulf of Guinea (Atlantic Ocean) to the Southwest, and to the west and northwest lies Nigeria.

For more information, please check this website:https://www. Africaguide.com/country/cameroon/

CAPE VERDE ISLANDS

Located in the Atlantic Ocean, 600 km (450 miles) west-northwest of Senegal, the Cape Verde Islands consist of Santo Antão, São Vicente, Santa Luzia, Ilheu Branco, Ilheu Raso, São Nicolau, Sal and Boa Vista, Maio, São Tiago, Fogo and Brava.

For more information, please check this website:https://www.Africaguide.com/country/ cverde/

CENTRAL AFRICAN REPUBLIC

As the name indicates, the Central African Republic lies in central Africa and is entirely within the tropical zone. Completely landlocked, it is bordered to the north by Chad, the east by Sudan, the south by Zaire and the Congo, and the west by Cameroon. The southern border follows the bed of the Ubangi River and the eastern border coincides with the divide between the watersheds of the Nile and the Zaire rivers.

For more information, please check this website:https://www.Africaguide.com/country/ car/

CHAD

Chad is a landlocked country located in Central Africa. Libya lies to the north, Niger and Nigeria to the west, Cameroon to the southwest, Central African Republic to the southeast and Sudan to the east.

For more information, please check this website:https://www.Africaguide.com/country/chad/

COMOROS

Climate: tropical marine; rainy season. (November to May)
Population: 850,856.
Area: 2,170 sq. km.

For more information, please check this website:https://www.Africaguide.com/comoros/

THE REPUBLIC OF CONGO

The Congo is located on the western coastline of Central Africa, bordering with the Southern Atlantic Ocean to the west, Angola to the south, Democratic Republic of the Congo (formerly Zaire) to the south and east, Central African Republic and Cameroon to the north, and Gabon to the northwest.

For more information, please check this website:https://www.Africaguide.com/congo/

DEMOCRATIC REPUBLIC OF THE CONGO

The Democratic Republic of the Congo (formerly Zaire) is situated in Central Africa and crosses the equator in the north-central region. The third largest country in Africa, it shares borders with Central African Republic to the north, Sudan to the northeast, Uganda, Rwanda, Burundi and Tanzania to the east, Zambia to the south and southeast, Angola to the southwest, and Angola and the Congo Republic to the west.

For more information, please check this website:https://www.Africaguide.com/zaire/

DJIBOUTI

Djibouti is located in Eastern Africa, bordering the Gulf of Aden and the Red Sea on the east, Eritrea to the north, Ethiopia to the north and northwest and Somalia to the southeast.

The country can be divided into three regions: the coastal plains and volcanic plateaus in the central and southern parts of the country and the mountain ranges in the north.

For more information, please check this website:https://www. Africaguide.com/djbouti/

EGYPT

Arguably one of the major tourist attractions in all of Africa, Egypt is bordered on the north by the Mediterranean Sea, the east by Israel and the Red Sea, the South by Sudan, and to the west by Libya.

The Nile delta is a broad alluvial land, sloping to the sea for 100 miles, with a 155-mile maritime front between Alexandria and Port Said. South of Cairo, most of the country (known as Upper Egypt) is a tableland rising to some 457m (1,500 ft), and the narrow valley of the Nile is enclosed by cliffs as high as 548m (1,800 ft). A series of cascades and rapids at Aswan, known as the First Cataract, forms a barrier to movement upstream.

For more information, please check this website:https://www. Africaguide.com/egypt/

EQUATORIAL GUINEA
- -

Equatorial Guinea lies on the west coast of Africa, bordering the North Atlantic Ocean, with Cameroon lying to the north and Gabon to the east and south.

For more information, please check this website: https://www. Africaguide.com/eguinea/

ERITREA
- -

Eritrea is located in north eastern Africa bordering with Ethiopia to the south, Sudan to the north, Djibouti to the southeast and the Red Sea to the east.

For more information, please check this website: https://www. Africaguide.com/eritrea/

ETHIOPIA
- -

Ethiopia is situated in the Horn of Africa, in the northeastern side of the continent bordering with Sudan to the north and north west, Eritrea to the north and north east, Djibouti to the east, Somalia to the east and south east and to the south lies Kenya.

For more information, please check this website: https://www. Africaguide.com/ethiopia/

GABON

Gabon is situated on the west coast of Africa and is bordered on the north by Cameroon, on the east and south by the Congo and the west by the Atlantic Ocean, on the northwest by Equatorial Guinea.

For more information, please check this website: https://www. Africaguide.com/gabon/

GAMBIA

Located on the west coast of Africa, Gambia is bordered by Senegal to the north, east and south and by the Atlantic Ocean to the west.

For more information, please check this website: https://www. Africaguide.com/gambia/

GHANA

Ghana is situated on the southern coast of the West African coast and is bordered to the east by Togo, to the west by the Ivory Coast, to the south by the Atlantic Ocean and to the north and northwest by Burkina Faso.

For more information, please check this website: https://www. Africaguide.com/ghana/

GUINEA BISSAU

Guinea-Bissau is situated on the west coast of Africa and is bordered to the north by Senegal, to the east and southeast by Guinea and to the west southwest by the Atlantic Ocean.

For more information, please check this website: https://www.Africaguide.com/guineab/

GUINEA

The Republic of Guinea, on the west coast of Africa is bordered to the north by Senegal and Mali and to the east by Mali and the Ivory Coast, to the south by Liberia and Sierra Leone, to the west by the Atlantic Ocean and to the northwest by Guinea-Bissau.

For more information, please check this website: https://www.Africaguide.com/guinea/

IVORY COAST [COTE D'IVOIRE]

The Republic of Ivory Coast, on the south coast of the western bulge of Africa, is bordered to the north by Mali and Burkina Faso, to the east by Ghana, to the south by the Gulf of Guinea of the Atlantic Ocean and to the west by Liberia and Guinea.

For more information, please check this website: https://www.Africaguide.com/ivoryc/

KENYA

Kenya lies astride the equator on the eastern coast of Africa. Kenya is bordered in the north by Sudan and Ethiopia, the east by Somalia, the southeast by the Indian Ocean, the southwest by Tanzania and the west by Lake Victoria and Uganda.

Kenya is notable for its geographical variety. The low-lying, fertile coastal region, fringed with coral reefs and islands, is backed by a gradually rising coastal plain, a dry region covered with savanna and thorn bush.

For more information, please check this website: https://www. Africaguide.com/kenya/

LESOTHO

Lesotho is enclosed by South Africa. Three distinct geographical regions, demarcated by ascending altitude, extend approximately north-south through the country. The western quarter of the country is a plateau averaging 5,000 ft to 6,000 ft, and ranges from a thin strip of 6 miles in width to a zone 40 miles wide. The soil of this zone is derived from sandstone and, particularly in the western most region, is poor and badly eroded.

For more information, please check this website: https://www. Africaguide.com/lesotho/

LIBERIA

Located on the west coast of Africa, Liberia is bordered by Guinea to the north, Ivory Coast to the east, Sierra Leone to the northwest and the Atlantic Ocean to the south and southwest.

For more information, please check this website:https://www.Africaguide.com/liberia/

LIBYA

Libya is situated on the coast of North Africa and is the fourth largest country on the continent. It borders with Egypt to the east, Sudan to the southeast, Chad and Niger to the south, Algeria to the west and Tunisia to the northwest and the Mediterranean Sea to the north.

For more information, please check this website: https://www.Africaguide.com/libya/

MADAGASCAR

Situated off the southeast coast of Africa, Madagascar is the fourth largest island in the world, covering an area of 590, 000 km. The climate varies greatly from one region to another: warm and rainy in the eastern part, temperate in the Highlands, warm and dry in the West, and very hot in the South. It is separated from the coast of Africa by the Mozambique Channel. The shortest distance between the island and the mainland is 400 km.

For more information, please check this website: https://www.Africaguide.com/madagas/

MALAWI

Climate: subtropical; rainy season (November to May); dry season (May to November).

Population: 18,628,747.

Area: 118,480 sq. km.

For more information, please check this website: https://www.Africaguide.com/malawi/

MALI

Climate: Tropical to arid.

Population: 19,658,031.

Area: 1,240,142 sq.km.

For more information, please check this website: https://www.Africaguide.com/mali/

MAURITIUS

Mauritius is an island located in the Indian Ocean about 800km (550 miles) east of Madagascar and 2,000 km (1,250 miles) off the nearest point of the African coast. The island of Rodrigues, an integral part of Mauritius, is located about 560 km (350 miles) off its northeastern coast.

For more information, please check this website: https://www.Africaguide.com/mauritan/

MAURITANIA

Situated in West Africa, Mauritania has borders with Algeria and Western Sahara to the northwest, Mali to the east and south, Senegal on the southwest and the Atlantic Ocean to the west.

There are three distinct geographic regions in Mauritania; a narrow belt along the Senegal River Valley in the south, where soil and climatic conditions permit settled agriculture.

For more information, please check this website: https://www. Africaguide.com/mauritis/

MOROCCO

Situated on the northwestern corner of Africa, Morocco shares borders with Algeria to the east and southeast, Mauritania to the south and to the west by the Atlantic Ocean.

The country is divided into three natural regions; the fertile northern coastal plains along the Mediterranean which contains Er Rif mountains varying in elevation up to about 8,000 ft; the plateaus and lowlands lying between the rugged Atlas Mountains, which extend in three parallel ranges from the Atlantic coast in the southwest to Algeria and the Mediterranean in the northeast; and the semiarid area in southern and eastern Morocco, which merges into the Sahara Desert. For more information, please check this website: https://www.Africaguide.com/morocco/

MOZAMBIQUE

Mozambique is located on the southeastern coast of Africa and rises toward the west to a plateau ranging from 500 ft to 2,000 ft above sea level and on the western border to a higher plateau (6,000 ft. to 8,000 ft.), with mountains in the north reaching a height of over 8,000 ft. The highest mountains are Namuli (7,936 ft.), Binga (7,992 ft) on the Zimbabwean border, and Serra Zuira (7,306 ft.) in Sofala Province.

For more information, please check this website: https://www.Africaguide.com/mozamb/

NAMIBIA

Namibia lies in Southwest Africa and borders the South Atlantic Ocean to the west, Angola to the north, Zambia to the northeast, Botswana to the southeast and South Africa to the south.

Namibia is the 34th largest country in the world. It stretches for 1,300km from south to north and varies from 480km to 930km in width from west to east.

For more information, please check this website: https://www.Africaguide.com/namibia/

NIGER

Niger is a landlocked country bordered in the north by Libya, Chad to the East, Nigeria to the south, Benin and Burkina Faso to the southwest, Mali to the west and Algeria to the northwest.

Two-thirds of Niger is desert with much of the northeastern part of the country uninhabitable. The remaining third of the country is savanna, suitable mainly for raising livestock and limited agriculture. In the north-central region is the volcanic Air Massif, attaining heights of up to 5,900 ft.

For more information, please check this website: https://www.Africaguide.com/niger/

NIGERIA

Nigeria is situated at the extreme inner corner of the Gulf of Guinea on the west coast of Africa. It shares borders with Chad to the northeast, Cameroon to the east, Benin to the west, Niger to the northwest and by the Atlantic Ocean (Gulf of Guinea) to the south.

For more information, please check this website: https://www. Africaguide.com/nigeria/

REUNION

Reunion lies in the Indian Ocean, approximately 220 km southwest of Mauritius and 800 km east of Madagascar.

The island is volcanic in origin and mountainous, and covers an area of 2,512 sq km (970 sq miles)

For more information, please check this website: https://www. Africaguide.com/reunion/

RWANDA

Landlocked and surrounded by Uganda in the north, Tanzania in the east, Burundi in the south, and Zaire to its west and northwest, Rwanda lies on the East African plateau, with the divide between the water systems of the Nile and Zaire rivers passing in a north-south direction through the western part of the country. For more information, please check this website: https://www.Africaguide. com/rwanda/

SAO THOME

Two main islands constitute the Democratic Republic of São Tomé and Principe and are a part of a chain of extinct volcanoes. Both islands are fairly mountainous and are situated in the Gulf of Guinea, straddling the Equator, west of mainland Gabon.

For more information, please check this website: https://www.Africaguide.com/sao_tome/

SENEGAL

With Mauritania on its northern and northeastern border, Mali to the east, Guinea and Guinea Bissau to the south and the Atlantic Ocean to the west, Senegal surrounds Gambia on three sides and is situated on the western bulge of Africa.

For more information, please check this website: https://www.Africaguide.com/senegal/

SEYCHELLES

The Seychelles is an archipelago in the Indian Ocean, northeast of Madagascar, consisting of more than 100 islands of which 83 are named and 46 are permanently uninhabited. Mahé is the principal island comprising of 142 sq km, with the islands of Praslin, La Digue and Silhouette being the most important. For more information, please check this website: https://www.Africaguide.com/seychel/

SIERRA LEONE

Sierra Leone shares borders with Guinea to the north and east, Liberia to the southeast, and the Atlantic Ocean to the south and west.

For more information, please check this website: https://www. Africaguide.com/sleone/

SOMALIA

Somalia is situated in the Horn of East Africa and is bordered by the Gulf of Aden and Djibouti to the north, the Indian Ocean to the east and south, to the north and northwest by Ethiopia and Kenya to the southwest.

For more information, please check this website: https://www. Africaguide.com/somalia/

SOUTH AFRICA

South Africa lies at the southernmost part of the African continent. It is bordered to the north by Botswana and Zimbabwe, to the northeast by Mozambique and Swaziland and to the northwest by Namibia. On the east coastline lies the Indian Ocean, the Southern coastline, the confluence of the Indian and Atlantic Oceans, and Atlantic Ocean on the western side. South Africa completely surrounds Lesotho.

For more information, please check this website: https://www. Africaguide.com/sAfrica/

SOUTH SUDAN

The capital city of South Sudan is Juba.

SUDAN

Situated in northeast Africa, Sudan borders with Egypt to the north, Ethiopia and Eritrea to the southeast, South Sudan to the south, the Central African Republic and Chad to the west and Libya to the northwest.

For more information, please check this website: https://www. Africaguide.com/sudan/

SWAZILAND [ESWATINI]

A landlocked country in southern Africa, Swaziland is bordered by Mozambique to the northeast and by South Africa to the southeast, south, west and north.

For more information, please check this website: https://www. Africaguide.com/swazi/

TANZANIA

Situated in East Africa, just south of the Equator, mainland Tanzania lies between the area of the great lakes: Victoria, Tanganyika and Malawi, with the Indian Ocean on its coastline to the east. It has land borders with Uganda and Kenya to the north, Mozambique and Malawi to the south, Zambia to the southwest and the Dem. Republic of Congo, Burundi and Rwanda to the west.

For more information, please check this website: https://www.Africaguide.com/tanzania/

TOGO

Situated on the west coast of Africa, Togo has land boundaries with Burkina Faso to the north, Benin to the east, Ghana to the west, and the south shares a border with the Gulf of Guinea (Atlantic Ocean).

For more information, please check this website: https://www.Africaguide.com/togo/

TUNISIA

Tunisia has boundaries with Algeria to the west, Libya to the southeast and the Mediterranean Sea to the north and east.

For more information, please check this website: https://www.Africaguide.com/tunisia/

UGANDA

Uganda is located in east-central Africa, situated north and northwest of Lake Victoria. It is a landlocked country bordered by Sudan to the North, Kenya to the east, Tanzania to the South, Rwanda to the southwest and Dem. Republic of the Congo to the northwest.

For more information, please check this website: https://www.Africaguide.com/uganda/

ZANZIBAR

Situated in the Indian Ocean, 36 km off the coastline of mainland Tanzania lies Zanzibar. Zanzibar officially refers to the archipelago that include Unguja and Pemba, surrounded by about 50 smaller ones.

For more information, please check this website: https://www. Africaguide.com/zanzibar/

ZAMBIA

Zambia is a landlocked country located between the southern rim of the Democratic Republic Congo Basin and the Zambezi River. Zambia has land borders with Tanzania to the northeast, Malawi to the east, Mozambique and Zimbabwe to the southeast, Botswana and Namibia to the south, Angola to the west and the Dem. Republic of Congo to the northwest.

For more information, please check this website: https://www. Africaguide.com/zambia/

ZIMBABWE

Zimbabwe is a landlocked country in south-central Africa. It lies between the Zambezi River to the north and the Limpopo River to the south. The country has land borders with Mozambique to the north and east, South Africa to the south, Botswana to the southwest and Zambia to the northwest and north.

For more information, please check this website: https://www. Africaguide.com/zimbab/

KOFI QUAYE

Kofi Quaye is a US based journalist and author. He has written and published books of fiction and nonfiction that focus on contemporary African culture. His books have been published by leading world class publishers including MacMillan Publishing Company. His published books of fiction and nonfiction include a number of collaborations with authors from. different backgrounds on a wide variety of subjects. FREE FROM DEATH ROAD was a collaboration with General Davis, a former upstate New York gang leader. MY TROUBLED LIFE was a collaboration with Mervyn Patrick about his life as a Trinidadian immigrant in America. He is a contributing editor to CNY VISION, a weekly newspaper in upstate New York.

PETER WYNN

Peter Wynn's expansive knowledge about the Caribbean and Africa uniquely qualifies him as a collaborator on this book. As a young American living in the Caribbean in the early eighties, his interaction with the people provided him with the insight on the global influence of African culture and the impact it has on people in different parts of the world. Traveling and experiencing life in Africa is one of his major goals.

Godfred Mensah is an author and a social entrepreneur based in Ghana. He has written extensively on subjects that explore the impact of culture on social and economic development in Africa. This is his third collaboration with Kofi Quaye. He made significant contributions to TRAPPED, a book on the immigrant experience and LOVE WITHOUT BORDERS, which focuses on relationships between people of different races and cultures.

Printed in the United States
By Bookmasters